全国职业技能英语系列教材

总主编 童敬东
总顾问 陆松岩

职场综合英语教程

第一册
（第二版）

主　编　童敬东
副主编　孙燕燕　张　珺
编　者　胡卫军　王　祎　袁春梅
　　　　刘湘屏　程建娥

Vocational
Comprehensive
English-Training
Course

北京大学出版社
PEKING UNIVERSITY PRESS

图书在版编目(CIP)数据

职场综合英语教程. 第一册/童敬东主编. —2版. —北京：北京大学出版社，2018.9
(全国职业技能英语系列教材)
ISBN 978-7-301-28604-3

Ⅰ.①职… Ⅱ.①童… Ⅲ.①英语–高等职业教育–教材 Ⅳ.①H319.39

中国版本图书馆CIP数据核字(2017)第195934号

书　　　名	职场综合英语教程 第一册(第二版) ZHICHANG ZONGHE YINGYU JIAOCHENG DI-YI CE
著作责任者	童敬东　主编
责 任 编 辑	郝妮娜
标 准 书 号	ISBN 978-7-301-28604-3
出 版 发 行	北京大学出版社
地　　　址	北京市海淀区成府路205号　100871
网　　　址	http://www.pup.cn　新浪微博:@北京大学出版社
电 子 信 箱	bdhnn2011@126.com
电　　　话	邮购部 010-62752015　发行部 010-62750672　编辑部 010-62759634
印 刷 者	北京大学印刷厂
经 销 者	新华书店
	787毫米×1092毫米　16开本　8.75印张　330千字 2012年8月第1版 2018年9月第2版　2018年9月第1次印刷
定　　　价	39.00元

未经许可，不得以任何方式复制或抄袭本书之部分或全部内容。
版权所有，侵权必究
举报电话: 010-62752024　电子信箱: fd@pup.pku.edu.cn
图书如有印装质量问题，请与出版部联系，电话: 010-62756370

第二版前言

《职场综合英语教程》自2012年出版以来经历了五个春秋。在此期间，高等职业教育的规模、生源、教学方法发生了新的变化。甚至针对高职高专设计的"高等学校英语应用能力考试"大纲和题型也有了明显的变化。基于此，在北京大学出版社的积极策划下，《职场综合英语教程》原分册主编积极沟通，并征求使用教材师生的意见，决定对原教材进行修订。

本次修订的原则是减少课文单元，降低课文难度，采用牛津词典常用音标，适当增加与高职高专英语技能大赛及最新"高等学校英语应用能力考试"（B级）题型相关的练习。修订主要体现在以下几个方面：

1. 基础篇保留六个单元框架，但更换了难度较大的篇章，使修订后的课文更贴近学生的英语水平。此外，所有音标改用牛津词典音标，与学生在中学阶段所学音标保持一致，更便于学生课前预习和教师组织课堂教学。

2. 第一册最明显的变化是删除两个话题较偏的单元，使原来的八个单元变成现在的六个单元。另外，与基础篇的修订方法相同，对所有生词采用牛津词典音标进行标注。

3. 第二册最明显的变化是压缩了原有单元，并对个别课文进行了降低难度的处理。与此同时，我们还对书中练习进行了修订，压缩或删除了部分实用性较弱的练习。这样做的目的是使本书内容更接近学生的学习能力，便于教师组织教学和调动学生的学习积极性。

4. 第三册秉承前几册的修订原则，对原书八个单元内容进行了压缩，删除了难度较大的篇章，保留了与职场关系度较高且难度适中的单元内容。所有生词的音标参照《牛津高阶英汉双解词典》（第七版）进行标注。此外，我们还对写作部分进行了必要的修订，剔除了与前几册重复的内容，增加了与职业技能大赛有关的话题。

五年来的教学实践证明，《职场综合英语教程》是一套严格按照国家职业教育目标和要求精心设计的高职高专公共英语教材，选材新颖，话题丰富，满足高职高专英语教学的实际需要。我们相信，修订后的这套教材更加符合高职高专教育对公共英语的教学要求，更加适合学习者的学习水平，更加有助于学生未来的职业发展。

编者
2017年7月

第一版前言

职业化已经成为高职高专教育最显著的特征。增加实训、强调动手能力、采用"订单式"培养模式是其主要特色。在这种背景下,按照传统的教学方法进行基础课教学已经不容置疑地受到了挑战。就目前情况论,高职高专的基础课教学必须践行"以服务为宗旨,以就业为导向"的专业建设指导思想。在课程建设以及基础课教学内容中,必须结合学生的专业需求,有意识地融入与职场相关联的知识。

根据教育部《高职高专英语教育课程教学基本要求》的精神,联合国家级示范高职院校和骨干高职院校的一线教师,在充分调查现有高职高专英语教材的基础上,结合高职英语教学的未来发展趋势,在"安徽省高职高专外语教研会"的组织及北京大学出版社的支持下,编写了本套《职场综合英语教程》,并被列入普通高等教育"十二五"规划教材。

本套教程分为基础篇、第一册、第二册和第三册,共四册。

基础篇 主要针对英语基础比较薄弱的学生,融入了对音标的训练,旨在帮助这部分学生巩固英语的基础知识,为后续课程的学习奠定必要的基础。

第一册 主要涉及西方文化和日常生活,内容涵盖西方名人、青年旅馆、主题公园、肥皂剧、网上购物等。鲜活的内容、生活化的主题,有利于学生顺利融入大学生活,同时也有助于培养学生对英语学习的兴趣,为今后的职业化过渡打下坚实基础。

第二册 主要涉及求职以及职业素养培养等主题,如求职、自主创业、职场中人际交往和做好服务、科技与生活、名人的成功与失败等。另外,本册内容与职场文化的有机融合有利于学生对未来职业规划形成初步的认识。

第三册 从职场生活出发,针对高职学生可能遇到的职场活动进行设计,内容包括机场接待、银行服务、汽车制造等。内容难度适中,选材谨慎,真正做到通识化与职场化有机统筹,有助于学生以后进一步学习相关的专业英语。

本套教材的内容主要分为六个方面:听说、阅读、语法、应用文写作、文化速递与拓展词汇。

听说部分 践行任务型教学的指导思想,强调能听懂简单对话,能记录关键词,能就所给事物说出英语名称,或进行角色分工,完成简单对话。这部分设计了热身环节,通过比较容易完成的任务,帮助学生尽快进入相关主题的学习。而角色扮演部分则试

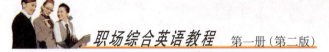

图充分调动学生的想象力和创造力,按照角色分工完成任务。听说部分还设计了听写内容,旨在培养学生听懂并记录关键词的能力。

阅读部分　　由两篇相关主题的文章组成,其中第一篇为主要文章,教师应该进行精深讲解;第二篇属于附加文章,教师可以把它作为泛读教材使用。目的是让学生在阅读过程中完成对该主题的英语核心词汇的巩固和学习,同时深刻理解英语的语句结构。

语法部分　　旨在夯实高职高专学生的语法基础,改善语法能力薄弱的现状,同时结合"高等学校英语应用能力考试"要求,对一些考试技巧进行精解,真正做到融会贯通,为提高英语综合能力打下良好基础。

写作部分　　紧扣职场,重在应用文的写作。提供较规范的写作模式与常用句型供学生参考,通过实际的操练让学生进一步熟悉并掌握多种应用文的写作。

文化速递　　是本套教材的特色之一。是针对单元主题的拓展性学习资料,可以帮助学生开阔视野、拓展知识面,提高综合人文素养。

词汇部分　　依据大纲要求,课文中涉及的生词均分级标出。标★为A级词汇,标☆为超纲词汇。方便教师把握教学重点,也方便学生分级掌握词汇,逐步晋级。

配有教学课件　　每个单元针对不同的主题都有话题的进一步延伸,有利于教师进行拓展教学。丰富授课内容,活跃课堂气氛,激发学生的学习兴趣。

本套教材得到教育部高等学校高职高专英语类专业教学指导委员会的悉心指导,由教指委秘书长牛健博士和副主任委员丁国声教授担任总顾问,由安徽新华学院外国语学院院长任静生教授担任总主编,国家示范性高等职业院校芜湖职业技术学院、安徽水利水电职业技术学院、安徽职业技术学院、安庆职业技术学院等院校的英语教学专家负责编写任务;明尼苏达大学商业管理Brian Meyer博士以及天津外国语大学等院校的专家为此套教材的出版倾注了大量的心血;其他参编人员及编辑老师们也付出了巨大的努力,在此谨向他们表示衷心的感谢。

高职高专英语教学任重道远,教材建设未有止境。本套教材的出版旨在探索新形势下高职高专英语教学的一条教学新路。缺点与不足之处在所难免,衷心希望得到专家学者的批评指正,听到广大师生的改进意见。

编者

2012年5月

Contents

Unit 1　Success Story ·· 1
    Part Ⅰ　　Listening and Speaking / 2
    Part Ⅱ　　Reading / 6
             Text A　Steve Jobs: "People with Passion Can Change the World" / 6
             Text B　Alibaba's Jack Ma: From "Crazy" to Be a Billionaire / 11
    Part Ⅲ　　Grammar Review 定语从句 / 15
    Part Ⅳ　　Applied Writing: Invitation（邀请信）/ 18
    Part Ⅴ　　Cultural Express: How Do You Like Jeremy Shu-How Lin / 20

Unit 2　Travelling ·· 23
    Part Ⅰ　　Listening and Speaking / 24
    Part Ⅱ　　Reading / 27
             Text A　Backpacking and Youth Hostels / 28
             Text B　Gap Year / 33
    Part Ⅲ　　Grammar Review 状语从句 / 36
    Part Ⅳ　　Applied Writing: Application Form（申请表）/ 40
    Part Ⅴ　　Cultural Express: Round-the-world Airline Ticket / 43

Unit 3　The English Language ··· 45
    Part Ⅰ　　Listening and Speaking / 46
    Part Ⅱ　　Reading / 50
             Text A　English Is a Queer Language / 50
             Text B　The Glorious Messiness of English / 55
    Part Ⅲ　　Grammar Review 主谓一致 / 59
    Part Ⅳ　　Applied Writing: Thank-you Letter（感谢信）/ 62
    Part Ⅴ　　Cultural Express: Crazy English / 64

Unit 4　Online Shopping 67
　　Part Ⅰ　Listening and Speaking / 68
　　Part Ⅱ　Reading / 72
　　　　　　Text A　Privacy and Security Issues in Online Shopping / 73
　　　　　　Text B　Some Benefits of Online Shopping / 78
　　Part Ⅲ　Grammar Review 倒装结构 / 81
　　Part Ⅳ　Applied Writing: Application Letter（求职信）/ 84
　　Part Ⅴ　Cultural Express: Students Start Online Grocery Store / 86

Unit 5　Advertisements 90
　　Part Ⅰ　Listening and Speaking / 91
　　Part Ⅱ　Reading / 95
　　　　　　Text A　The Most Effective Advertising of All / 95
　　　　　　Text B　How to Create an Advertisement / 100
　　Part Ⅲ　Grammar Review 虚拟语气 / 104
　　Part Ⅳ　Applied Writing: E-mail（电子邮件）/ 107
　　Part Ⅴ　Cultural Express: Coca-Cola Advertising Stories / 109

Unit 6　Theme Parks 112
　　Part Ⅰ　Listening and Speaking / 113
　　Part Ⅱ　Reading / 116
　　　　　　Text A　Visiting Theme Parks / 117
　　　　　　Text B　Walt Disney / 122
　　Part Ⅲ　Grammar Review 被动语态 / 126
　　Part Ⅳ　Applied Writing: Notice（通知）/ 128
　　Part Ⅴ　Cultural Express: Indoor Water Parks / 130

Unit 1

Success Story

Learning Objectives

You are able to:
- Introduce yourself
- Introduce a good friend of yours to others
- Talk about famous persons
- Comment on success or failure
- Listen for key words and useful expressions
- Learn to use attributive clause correctly
- Write an invitation

You are suggested to:
- Recite wisdoms
- Be familiar with famous persons

Part I Listening and Speaking

Warm-up

Task 1

Directions: Can you figure out the names of the famous persons in the pictures? If you have difficulties, please turn to the Internet or your partner for help.

(1)　　　　　(2)　　　　　(3)　　　　　(4)

(5)　　　　　(6)　　　　　(7)　　　　　(8)

Oprah Winfrey	David Beckham	Audrey Hepburn
William Shakespeare	Vladimir Vladimirovich Putin	
Stephen William Hawking	Elvis Presley(King)	Barack Obama

Task 2

Directions: Read the following wisdoms loudly. Work with your partner and guess their meanings.

1. Activity is the only road to knowledge. —Bernard Shaw
2. The empty vessels make the greatest sound. —Shakespeare
3. Reading makes a full man, conference a ready man, and writing an exact man. —Bacon
4. The important thing in life is to have a great aim, and the determination to attain it. —Goethe
5. If winter comes, can spring be far behind? —Shelley

6. Where there is a will, there is a way. —Edison
7. Early to bed and early to rise, makes a man healthy, wealthy and wise. —Franklin
8. All the splendor in the world is not worth a good friend. —Voltaire
9. Ordinary people merely think how they shall spend their time; a man of talent tries to use it. —Schopenhauer
10. It is no use doing what you like ; you have got to like what you do. —Churchill

Oral Practice

Task 1

Directions: Read and practise the following dialogue with your partner, then mark the following statements with "T" or "F" according to what you have read.

Mary: David, I would like to introduce my teacher Miss Smith to you. Shall we go and see her now?
David: Good. Let's go.
Mary: Miss Smith, this is my friend David. David, this is my teacher Miss Smith.
Smith: Hi, David.
David: Hi, Miss Smith. I'm glad to meet you.
Smith: I'm glad to meet you, too. Are you and Mary in the same class?
David: No. I'm in Mr. Brown's class.
Mary: Miss Smith, David is a very good soccer player and he has played it for years.
Smith: Has he? I like watching soccer games.
David: Will you come and watch us play some day, Miss Smith?
Smith: Yes, I will. Thank you.

_____ 1. David and Mary are schoolmates.
_____ 2. The conversation probably takes place at Miss Smith's office.
_____ 3. Mary says that David is a very good student.
_____ 4. Miss Smith says that she seldom watches soccer games.
_____ 5. David would like to go and visit Miss Smith again some day.

Task 2

Directions: Use the information given below to create a role-play.

Introduce yourself to your class. Then get to know two or three fellow students. Take notes on the information you get from them and prepare to introduce them to your class. You may begin with:

Allow me to introduce myself. I'm ...
Let me introduce myself. My name is ...
May I have the pleasure of introducing ... to you?
I'd like to introduce ... to you.

Listening Practice

Task 1

Directions: Now you will hear five short conversations. They will be read only once. After each conversation, there is a question. Listen carefully and choose the best answer from the four choices.

1. ☐ music   ☐ chemistry   ☐ sports   ☐ fashion
2. ☐ The woman might become a famous movie star in the end.
   ☐ The woman is unlikely to become a movie star.
   ☐ The woman is as ugly as a pig.
   ☐ The woman will succeed soon.
3. ☐ She wants the man to cheer up.   ☐ She wants the man to work hard.
   ☐ She wants the man to take a rest.   ☐ She wants the man to be careful.
4. ☐ Brother and sister.   ☐ Father and daughter.
   ☐ Husband and wife.   ☐ Mother and son.
5. ☐ In a class of politics.   ☐ In a class of literature.
   ☐ In a class of math.   ☐ In a class of arts.

Task 2

Directions: Now you will hear a long conversation. It will be read twice. Then you are required to answer the following questions by making correct choices.

1. Who is good at 110 hurdle?
   ☐ Liu Xiang.   ☐ Wang Hao.
2. What kind of famous people does Zhou like?
   ☐ Sports stars.   ☐ Movie stars.
3. What kind of people can be regarded as famous people according to Zhou?
   ☐ Those with a lot of fans.
   ☐ Those who have great achievements for our society.

Unit 1 Success Story

Task 3

Directions: Now you will hear a short passage. It will be read three times. Then you are required to put in the missing information.

Money, _____, and attention often come with fame. For some people, these things have a corrupting influence. They cling to their fame, seek to _____, and stop being creative. This wasn't the case with Marie Curie, one of _____ in history.

Curie became the first woman to win a Nobel Prize _____. This did not _____ continuing to work and make even more discoveries and inventions. For her ceaseless efforts and _____, Curie earned her second Nobel Prize in 1911. She was the first person ever to receive two Nobel Prizes. Fame was never a burden to Curie.

New Words and Expressions

soccer	/ˈsɒkə/	n.	足球
hurdle	/ˈhɜːdl/	n.	栏杆,障碍
athlete	/ˈæθliːt/	n.	运动员
reasonable	/ˈriːznəbəl/	adj.	通情达理的
contribution	/ˌkɒntrɪˈbjuːʃn/	n.	贡献
achievement	/əˈtʃiːvmənt/	n.	成就
genius	/ˈdʒiːniəs/	n.	天才,天赋;天才人物
inspiration	/ˌɪnspəˈreɪʃn/	n.	灵感
perspiration	/ˌpɜːspəˈreɪʃn/	n.	汗水,流汗
corrupt	/kəˈrʌpt/	v.	腐蚀,使堕落
cling	/klɪŋ/	v.	(to) 紧紧抓(抱)住;挨近
creative	/kriːˈeɪtɪv/	adj.	创造(性)的
discovery	/dɪˈskʌvərɪ/	n.	被发现的事物
invention	/ɪnˈvenʃn/	n.	发明(物)
ceaseless	/ˈsiːsləs/	adj.	不绝的,不停的
burden	/ˈbɜːdn/	n.	重担,负荷

Nobel Prize

诺贝尔奖是以瑞典著名的化学家、硝化甘油炸药的发明人阿尔弗雷德·贝恩哈德·诺贝尔的部分遗产(3100万瑞典克朗)作为基金创立的。诺贝尔奖分设物理、化学、生理或医学、文学、和平五个奖项,以基金每年的利息或投资收益授予前一年世界上在这些领域对人类做出重大贡献的人,1901年首次颁发。诺贝尔奖包括金质奖章、证书和奖金。

Part II Reading

Text A

Before Reading:

1. The famous persons in the pictures below are well-known in China. Please say something about them (for example, their names, their career and their great achievements).

(1)　　　　(2)　　　　(3)　　　　(4)

(5)　　　　(6)　　　　(7)　　　　(8)

2. Different people have different ideas about what success is. What's your opinion about success? How do your classmates define it?

(useful words: money, power, happiness, love, friendship, freedom, achievement, popularity)

Steve Jobs: "People with Passion Can Change the World"

When Steve Jobs took a medical leave of absence from Apple, people talked about the role passion played throughout his life and what passion means to today's leaders.

Steve Jobs was one of the most important people in launching the personal computer era at the beginning of his time with Apple. When he returned to Apple in 1997, he launched the post-PC era.

Unit 1 Success Story

He returned to Apple after a 12-year absence from the company he had founded. Apple was close to bankruptcy at the time. Over the next decade Jobs not only changed the company, but turned it into one of the most important brands of our time. In those first months when Apple employees and investors were not sure of the future, Jobs held an informal staff meeting. What he told his employees sounds as true today as it did then:

"Marketing is about values. This is a very complicated world. It's a very noisy world. We're not going to get a chance for people to remember a lot about us. No company is. So we have to be really clear about what we want our customers to know about us. Our customers want to know what we stand for. What we're about is not simply helping people to get their jobs done, although we do that very well. Apple is about more than that. We believe that people with passion can change the world for the better. That's what we believe."

There are many individuals who are financially successful although they are not passionate about their jobs or their companies. But those who are truly "inspiring" are really passionate. What are they passionate about? They are not passionate about their products. They are passionate about what their products mean to the lives of their customers. They are passionate about how their products or services improve the world. Steve Jobs is very successful and inspiring not because he makes great computers, phones and MP3 players. He's inspiring because he's passionate about his customers and their ability to change the world when using his products.

In 2005, Jobs gave a famous speech to Stanford graduates. He said, "Your time is limited, so don't waste it living someone else's life. Stay hungry. Stay foolish." Remember those words because, as a leader, your best days are ahead if you remain passionate about your brand and its benefit to the world.

New Words

（标★为A级词汇，标☆为超纲词汇）

medical	/ˈmedɪkl/	adj.	医学的，医疗的，医术的
★passion	/ˈpæʃn/	n.	热情
throughout	/θruːˈaʊt/	adv.	遍及；自始至终
★launch	/lɔːntʃ/	v.	发射；创立
★era	/ˈɪərə/	n.	时代
post-PC	/ˌpəʊstpiːˈsiː/	n.	后PC时代
found	/faʊnd/	v.	建立
☆bankruptcy	/ˈbæŋkrʌptsɪ/	n.	破产
decade	/ˈdekeɪd/	n.	十年
★brand	/brænd/	n.	品牌
employee	/ɪmˈplɔɪiː/	n.	雇工，雇员

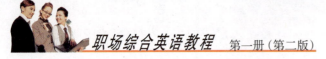

investor	/ɪnˈvestə/	n.	投资者
informal	/ɪnˈfɔːml/	adj.	非正式的,非正规的
★ staff	/stɑːf/	n.	全体职员
marketing	/ˈmɑːkɪtɪŋ/	n.	销售
★ complicated	/ˈkɒmplɪkeɪtɪd/	adj.	结构复杂的
customer	/ˈkʌstəmə/	n.	顾客
★ individual	/ˌɪndɪˈvɪdʒʊəl/	n.	个人
★ financially	/faɪˈnænʃəlɪ/	adv.	金融地
☆ passionate	/ˈpæʃənət/	adj.	热切的
★ inspiring	/ɪnˈspaɪərɪŋ/	adj.	赋予灵感的
product	/ˈprɒdʌkt/	n.	产品;产物
improve	/ɪmˈpruːv/	v.	改善,改进,提高
ahead	/əˈhed/	adv.	在前面,向前
benefit	/ˈbenɪfɪt/	n.	利益,好处

Phrases and Expressions

| close to | 接近于;在近处 |
| stand for | 代表;主张 |

Proper Names

Steve Jobs	史蒂夫·乔布斯
Apple	苹果公司
PC	个人电脑
MP3	一种音频压缩格式(Moving Picture Experts Group Audio Layer-3)
Stanford	(此处指)斯坦福大学

Exercises

I. Reading Comprehension

Directions: Answer the questions or complete the statements by choosing A, B, C, or D according to the text.

1. What is the passage mainly about?
   A. Steve Jobs' success in founding Apple.
   B. Steve Jobs' achievements and the role passion played throughout his life.
   C. Steve Jobs' important role in Apple Inc.
   D. Steve Jobs' life and his speech at Stanford University.

2. Steve Jobs made a lot of contributions but he didn't _____.
   A. develop such famous brands as ipad and iphone
   B. turn Apple into one of the most important brands in our time
   C. launch the personal computer era at the beginning of his time with Apple
   D. change Apple when it was close to bankruptcy
3. What does Jobs mean by saying "Stay hungry. Stay foolish." in his famous speech to Stanford graduates?
   A. You should not eat too much or be clever.
   B. You should be curious about the world.
   C. You should be passionate about the brand and its benefit to the world.
   D. You should be full of ambition.
4. Which of the following statements is TRUE according to the passage?
   A. Diligence plays an important role in getting to success.
   B. Jobs did not leave Apple before 1997.
   C. People who are truly "inspiring" are those who are financially successful.
   D. Steve Jobs made a lot of products, including MP3 players.
5. Steve Jobs is successful because he _____.
   A. made great computers, phones and MP3 players
   B. worked harder than others
   C. was passionate about his customers and their ability to change the world when using his products
   D. founded Apple and made many useful products

II. Identifying Pictures

Directions: Match each famous person in the picture with his or her name.

(1)　　　　(2)　　　　(3)　　　　(4)

(5)　　　　(6)　　　　(7)　　　　(8)

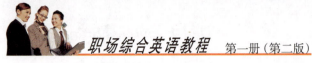

( ) Albert Einstein ( ) Kobe Bean Bryant Cox ( ) Lady Gaga
( ) Ernest Miller Hemingway ( ) Bill Gates ( ) Michael Phelps
( ) Michael Jackson ( ) Vincent van Gogh

III. Blank Filling

Directions: Use the following words or expressions in the box to translate parts of the following sentences.

| talk about | stand for | play an important role in | passion | |
| close to | inspire | financial | launch | era | brand |

1. Parents _____ （对于孩子的学习起重要作用）.
2. The company hopes to _____ （推出这种新药）by next October.
3. As a traffic signal, the red light _____ （代表"停止"）.
4. The beautiful scenery _____ （给了他灵感而创造出他最伟大的诗篇）.
5. Although the temperature falls, _____ （出游的热情）heats up.
6. Tokyo and New York are _____ （主要的金融中心）.
7. We spent the rest of the evening laughing, listening to country music and _____
_____ （谈论我们的将来）.
8. _____ （什么牌子的牙膏）do you prefer?
9. I don't mind where we go on vacation as long as it's _____ （靠近海滩）.
10. His death marked _____ （时代的结束）.

IV. True or False

Directions: Tell whether the following statements are true or false. Write "T" if the statement is true and "F" if it is false.

_____ 1. Steve Jobs launched the post-PC era when Apple was close to bankruptcy.
_____ 2. In 1985, Jobs left Apple, which he had founded.
_____ 3. According to Jobs, people who work hard can change the world.
_____ 4. According to Steve Jobs, people cannot succeed without being passionate about their jobs.
_____ 5. Passion plays an important role in Steve Jobs' success throughout his life.

Text B

Before Reading:

1. Who is Jack Ma? Say something about him and his company.
2. Before he became successful, Jack Ma was called "Crazy Jack Ma". What is your opinion about this nickname?

Alibaba's Jack Ma: From "Crazy" to Be a Billionaire

Jack Ma, founder and chairman of Alibaba, is one of those self-made billionaires in the technology field. He believed in the Internet's business potential when few other Chinese did. Outlandish ideas earned him the nickname "Crazy Jack Ma." But no one thinks he's mad now.

Starting at age 12, Ma awoke at 5 a.m. to walk or bicycle to Hangzhou's main hotels so he could practice English with foreign tourists. He did this for nine years and acted as a free tour guide to many foreigners.

Graduating in 1988, Ma taught English at a local college for five years. During that time, he also applied for, and failed to land, jobs at a local KFC, a hotel and the city police.

Determined to enter business, he set up a translation company, but he still had to sell goods on the street to get by. Ma traveled to the United States in 1995 as a translator. When he searched for "beer" and "China" during his first use of the Internet, Ma found nothing. But there was plenty of information about American and German beer.

Sensing an opportunity, Ma built a Chinese-language web page. Within hours of launch, he was receiving inquiries from around the world. The Internet, Ma thought, is "going to change the world and change China."

A few years later, in 1999, Ma gathered 17 friends at his home. They worked on a new venture: a website to connect exporters with foreign buyers. Alibaba.com was born. The firm quickly outgrew Ma's apartment, eventually becoming the dominant tech company in China.

Ma resigned in 2013 as Alibaba's CEO, but he clearly remains in charge as the firm's executive chairman. He has hinted at exploring more "cultural" pursuits, such as film-making, education and environmental protection.

Ma believes in both Buddhism and Taoism, and his hero is Forrest Gump. By

Ma's own account, "Forrest Gump never gives up and believes in what he is doing." He also likes the phrase "Life is like a box of chocolates because you never know what you're gonna get."

New Words

（标★为A级词汇，标☆为超纲词汇）

☆billionaire	/ˌbɪljəˈneə/	n.	亿万富翁
self-made	/ˌselfˈmeɪd/	adj.	白手起家的；靠自己奋斗成功的
potential	/pəˈtenʃl/	adj.	潜在的，可能的
		n.	潜力，潜质
☆outlandish	/aʊtˈlændɪʃ/	adj.	极不寻常的；奇特的
nickname	/ˈnɪkneɪm/	n.	绰号，外号
local	/ˈləʊkl/	adj.	地方的，当地的
land	/lænd/	v.	成功得到；着陆
determined	/dɪˈtɜːmɪnd/	adj.	决心；决定
plenty	/ˈplenti/	n.	大量；众多
within	/wɪˈðɪn/	prep.	在（某段时间）内
★inquiry	/ɪnˈkwaɪəri/	n.	查问；查询
venture	/ˈventʃə/	n.	企业，商业；经营项目
★exporter	/ekˈspɔːtə/	n.	出口商；出口公司
☆outgrow	/ˌaʊtˈɡrəʊ/	v.	增长得容不进（某地）；比……长得高（或大）
eventually	/ɪˈventʃuəli/	adv.	最后，终于
★dominant	/ˈdɒmɪnənt/	adj.	首要的，占优势的
tech	/tek/	n.	科技
☆resign	/rɪˈzaɪn/	v.	辞职，辞去（职务）
charge	/tʃɑːdʒ/	n.	收费；指控
		v.	收（费）；控告；给……充电
★executive	/ɪɡˈzekjətɪv/	n.	（公司或机构的）主管领导，管理人员
hint	/hɪnt/	v.	暗示，透露
explore	/ɪkˈsplɔː/	v.	勘探；探索
pursuit	/pəˈsjuːt/	n.	追求，寻找；爱好
account	/əˈkaʊnt/	n.	账户；描述；解释
phrase	/freɪz/	n.	短语；警句
gonna	/ˈɡɒnə, ˈɡɔːnə/		即将，将要（非正式用语，等于going to）

Phrases and Expressions

act as	充当；起作用
apply for	申请
get by	维持生计
believe in	相信某人(某事物)存在；认为某事好；信任

Proper Names

Alibaba		阿里巴巴
Jack Ma		马云
KFC		肯德基
Buddhism	/ˈbʊdɪzəm/	佛教
Taoism	/ˈtaʊɪzəm/	道教
Forrest Gump		阿甘
CEO		首席执行官

Exercises

I. Summary

Directions: Fill in the blanks with the exact words in the passage according to your understanding.

Jack Ma is the (1) _____ and chairman of Alibaba. In (2) _____, he traveled to the (3) _____ and used the Internet for the first time. A few years later, he and 17 partners set up a new (4) _____, a business to business platform, which connected (5) _____ with foreign buyers. Now Alibaba has become the (6) _____ tech company in China.

Ma is now still the (7) _____ of Alibaba. He shows interests in exploring more cultural pursuits, such as film-making, (8) _____ and environmental protection.

Ma believes in both (9) _____ and Taoism. His hero is Forrest Gump. He also likes the phrase "Life is like a box of (10) _____ because you never know what you're gonna get."

II. Comprehension Based on the Text

Directions: Complete the following two statements based on the text.

1. When he was 12 years old, Ma used to get up very early to _____ to Hangzhou's main hotels in order to practice English with foreigners.
2. Forrest Gump is regarded as a hero by Ma because he never _____ and believes in what he is doing.

III. Vocabulary & Structures

Directions: Choose the proper words or expresions in the box and fill in the blanks.

| potential | fail | pursuit | plenty of | practice |
| during | apply for | connect | opportunity | determined |

1. Wages have fallen by more than twenty percent _____ the past two months.
2. The new bridge _____ the surrounding villages with the town.
3. We are aware of the _____ problems and have taken every precaution（措施）.
4. If you are _____ to do something, you have made a firm decision to do it and will not let anything stop you.
5. Millions of people have tried to loose weight and _____ miserably.
6. If you want to _____ a job at the office where I work, I'll put in a good word for you.
7. Many busy executives have begun to _____ yoga（瑜伽）and meditation（冥想）.
8. When we were finally alone, I took the _____ to ask him a few personal questions.
9. There are _____ materials you can choose from; the problem now is how to make your selection.
10. People are having to move to other areas in _____ of work.

IV. Translation

Directions: Put the following English sentences into Chinese.

1. He believed in the Internet's business potential when few other Chinese did.
2. When he searched for "beer" and "China" during his first use of the Internet, Ma found nothing.
3. But there was plenty of information about American and German beer.
4. They worked on a new venture: a website to connect exporters with foreign buyers.
5. Life is like a box of chocolates because you never know what you're gonna get.

Part III Grammar Review

定语从句

定语从句通常位于所修饰的名词或代词之后，在句中充当定语。被定语从句修饰的词叫先行词。引导定语从句的连接词有关系代词(that, which, who, whom, whose)和关系副词(where, when, why)。关系代词在定语从句中作主语、宾语或定语。关系副词在定语从句中作状语，如：

The audience which is composed entirely of students is larger than ever.

全部由学生组成的观众人数比以前多。

解释：关系代词which的先行词是audience，在定语从句中which作主语。

The small countryside in which I lived was a beautiful place.

我过去生活过的小乡村是个很漂亮的地方。

解释：关系代词which的先行词是small countryside，在定语从句中which作介词in的宾语。

At the meeting, there are several people whose names I do not know.

会上有几个人我叫不出名字。

解释：关系代词whose的先行词是several people，在定语从句中whose作名词names的定语。

I'll never forget the day when I first met you.

我永远不会忘记第一次遇见你的那天。

解释：关系副词when的先行词是day。在定语从句中，when作时间状语，修饰定语从句中谓语动词met。

That is the factory where I worked three years ago.

那就是我三年前工作过的工厂。

解释：关系副词where的先行词是factory。在定语从句中，where作地点状语，修饰定语从句中谓语动词worked。

注意：which 和 that 指物时可互换，但在下列情况下必须用that：

① 先行词前有最高级形容词修饰

It was the largest map that I ever saw. 这是我见过的最大的地图。

This is the most expensive picture I bought. 这是我买过的最贵的一幅画。

② 先行词被all, any, no, only, little, much, last, very 或序数词所修饰，或先行词是all, much, nothing, something, little, anything, few 时。

This is the only bathroom that belongs to us. 只有这个卫生间是我们的。

Many trees that are in the park were planted last year.

公园里的很多树是去年栽的。

Have you taken down everything that Mr. Smith has said?

你把史密斯先生说的内容都记下来了吗？

There seems to be nothing that seems impossible for him in the world.

对他来说世界上似乎没有做不成的事。

There is little that I can do for you. 我对你真是爱莫能助。

This is one of the most exciting football games that I have ever seen.

这是我看过的最激动人心的一次足球比赛。

③ 当先行词既有人又有物时

The people and things that I saw during my visit to the city left a deep impression on me.

在我访问期间，那个城市的人和事给我留下了深刻的印象。

The report made no mention of the men and the cars that disappeared in the storm.

报告没提风暴中失踪的人和车。

定语从句因其与先行词之间的关系程度分为限制性定语从句和非限制性定语从句两种。限制性定语从句一般不能与所修饰的先行词分开，具有明确的限制功能；非限制性定语从句不像限制性定语从句那样与先行词关系密切，对它有很强的修饰和限制作用；非限制性定语从句一般只对所修饰的词作进一步的解释，如果去掉，并不影响句子的主要含义，因此常用逗号与先行词分开。

Those who/that have finished their homework can go home now.

已完成作业的人可以回家了。

解释：本句使用了限制性定语从句，表示"那些完成作业的人可以回家"，含有"那些没完成作业的人不能回家"之意。

We first went to Guilin, where we stayed for two days, and then went to Kunming.

我们首先去桂林，待上两天，然后去昆明。

解释：本句使用了非限制性定语从句，如果把该从句去掉，句子的主要含义并不受多大影响。

对于非限制性定语从句而言，先行词指人时，引导词用关系代词who或whom；先行词指物时，引导词用关系代词which（不能用that）；先行词指时间或地点时，引导词用关系副词when或where。如：

• Unit 1   Success Story •

In this factory a worker, who works six hours a day, earns more than 3000 yuan a month.
在这家工厂，工人每天劳动六个小时，一个月可挣到3000多元。
That river, which is 700 miles long, is in Guangdong.
这条江蜿蜒700英里，位于广东省境内。
Let's go to the Great Wall next week, when we won't be very busy.
下周不太忙，我们去爬长城吧。

Assignment

Directions: There are ten incomplete statements here. You are required to complete each statement by choosing the appropriate answer from the four choices marked A, B, C, and D.

1. The man _____ visited our school yesterday is from London.
   A. who   B. which   C. whom   D. when
2. He talked about a hero _____ no one had ever heard.
   A. about that   B. from whom   C. of whom   D. who
3. Have you read the book _____ I lent to you?
   A. that   B. whom   C. when   D. whose
4. Do you work near the building _____ colour is yellow?
   A. that   B. which   C. its   D. whose
5. Do you know the reason _____ she has changed her mind?
   A. which   B. why   C. that   D. when
6. I shall never forget those years _____ I lived in the country with the farmers, _____ has a great effect on my life.
   A. that; which B. when; which   C. which; that   D. when; who
7. _____ was expected, he succeeded in the exam.
   A. It   B. Which   C. As   D. That
8. He studied hard and later became a well-known writer, _____ his father expected.
   A. that was what   B. what was that
   C. and which was   D. which was what
9. Just before 9 o'clock on Sunday evening 28 May, 1967, Chichester arrived back in England, _____ a quarter of a million people were waiting to welcome him.
   A. which   B. where   C. when   D. how
10. You must do everything _____ I have told you to.
    A. that   B. which   C. when   D. how

Part IV Applied Writing

Invitation（邀请信）

邀请信可分为正式邀请和非正式邀请。正式邀请也叫请柬，多用于正式的大型活动，如：邀请参加学术会议、访问考察、讲学、婚礼等。非正式邀请用于朋友之间，如：邀请朋友吃饭、喝茶、看电影等。写邀请信时语言应简短、热情，并详细说明邀请的目的、时间和地点。

邀请信的主要内容：1.表明写作意图，向对方发出邀请；2.说明邀请的具体原因，活动的具体时间及地点等；3结尾时表示希望对方接受邀请；4.表明希望尽快得到答复，有时可注明R.S.V.P./r.s.v.p.（法语，意思是"请赐复"）。

邀请信回复的主要内容：1.无论是否接受邀请，都应表明谢意；2.如接受邀请，应确认应邀时间、地点等详细信息；3.如谢绝邀请，文字应婉转，并表示歉意，说明原因。

Sample 1 (邀请)

Dec. 16th, 2016

Dear Mr. Black,

　　We would like to invite you and your wife to attend our English evening party on December 24, 2016, from 7:30 to 9:30 p.m. We look forward to hearing from you soon.

　　　　　　　　　　　　　　　　　　　　　　Yours sincerely,
　　　　　　　　　　　　　　　　　　　　　　David Li
　　　　　　　　　　　　　　　　　　　　　　Monitor of Chemistry Class

Sample 2 (接受邀请)

Dec. 20th, 2016

Dear David Li,

　　Thank you very much for your letter of December 16th inviting us to come to your English evening party. We are very pleased to accept and will be there on time. Looking forward to seeing you.

　　　　　　　　　　　　　　　　　　　　　　Yours sincerely,
　　　　　　　　　　　　　　　　　　　　　　Ted & Mary Black

Sample 3 (拒绝邀请)

Dec. 20th, 2016
Dear David Li,
Thank you very much for your kind invitation to attend your English evening party. Unfortunately, we have already decided to go to Hong Kong on December 20th. We are sorry that we will not be able to come. We do appreciate your inviting us and hope that we will have the opportunity to attend your party next time.
Yours sincerely,
Ted & Mary Black

◆ 邀请信常用句型

We hope you can come and look forward to seeing you.
我们希望你能来,并期待着与你见面。

We are expecting with great pleasure to see you.
我们怀着愉快的心情期待着与你相见。

I hope you won't decline my invitation.
我希望你不要拒绝我的邀请。

We are waiting for your arrival.
我们等待着你的到来。

We sincerely hope you can attend ...
我们衷心希望你能来参加……

It gives me the greatest pleasure to invite you to visit this exhibition.
能邀请您参观展览是我最大的荣幸。

We look forward to hearing from you soon.
希望不久就能收到你的回信。

I really hope you can make it.
真的希望您能设法前来。

Please confirm your participation at your earliest convenience.
是否参加,请早日告知。

◆ 回复邀请常用句型

Please accept my sincere regrets for not being able to join ...
我不能参加……了,请接受我真诚的歉意。

I regret that I have another engagement on that day and will not be able to attend.
十分抱歉,我届时另有约会,故不能出席。

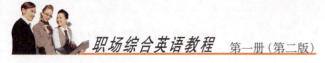

Assignment

Directions: This part is to test your ability to do practical writing. You are required to write an invitation and a reply based on the following information given in Chinese.

1. 给Jack写一封邀请信。请他于11月25日晚6:00前往你家吃晚饭,饭后将举行舞会,希望他参加。要求回复告知是否能参加。
2. 张玲教授邀请John Scott先生去他们学校做报告,题目是"Cultural Shock"。请你以John Scott先生的身份给张玲教授写封回信,表示愿意接受邀请。

Part V Cultural Express

How Do You Like Jeremy Shu-How Lin

The story of Jeremy Lin has caught on like wildfire with basketball fans around the world.

From such online news as "Just Lin, 10 Lessons Jeremy Lin Can Teach Us Before We Go To Work" to crazy auction sales for his high school yearbook autograph, Lin's fame has caught the attention of the media like few NBA players before him.

Jeremy Lin, whose full name is Jeremy Shu-How Lin, works for New York Knicks(尼克斯队) as a Point Guard(控球后卫). He was born in Los Angeles, California and graduated from Harvard.

How do you like him? Below are some facts and information about Jeremy Lin. I know you will like it.

1. Lin is now living with his brother. He has been looking around for his own house now that he has a contract for the rest of the season, but for now, Lin's residence is on his older brother Joshua's couch. Joshua is an NYU(纽约大学)student.

2. Lin is the first American-born NBA player of Chinese descent. There have been others of Asian descent (such as Yao Ming) and other Asian Americans, but Lin has broken new ground.

3. Lin's No. 17 has been the NBA's top online seller since Feb. 4. Lin burst onto the scene that day with a 25-point effort in New York's 99-92 win over the New Jersey Nets(新泽西网队).

4. Lin hopes to become a pastor when his playing days end. Lin is not shy about his religion.

5. As Lin's star has risen, so have his Twitter(微博客)followers. More than 210,000

people now follow @JLin7 on Twitter-up from just 82,000 people a week ago. All for the right to see Lin tweet: "This team is so unselfish and has so much heart. Love playing with them!"

6. Lin sent a DVD and resume to several school in the Ivy League(常春藤联盟) in order to attract recruiting interest, but he was only offered a walk-on role by UCLA(加州大学洛杉矶分校) and Stanford. Lin chose to attend Harvard at last, although the school does not offer scholarships.

7. Lin is now with his third NBA team. As a beginner, Lin was signed by his hometown Golden State Warriors(金州勇士队) to a two-year contract. He spent a season on the bench in San Francisco, appearing in only 29 games while averaging 2.6 points per game.

8. Lin can read China's major language Mandarin, and speaks enough of it to answer some questions. Lin's sudden popularity is quite inspiring. Who will become the next?

拓展词汇

福布斯名人榜

Oprah Winfrey 奥普拉·温弗; Beyonce Knowles 碧昂斯·诺里斯; James Cameron 詹姆斯·卡梅隆; Tiger Wood 泰格·伍兹; Britney Spears 布兰妮·斯皮尔斯; Johnny Depp 约翰尼·德普; Madonna 麦当娜; Taylor Swift 泰勒·斯威夫特; Kobe Bryant 科比·布莱恩特; Angelina Jolie 安吉丽娜·朱莉; Michael Jordan 迈克尔·乔丹; Steven Spielberg 史蒂芬·斯皮尔伯格

欧美娱乐节目

The Oprah Winfrey Show 奥普拉脱口秀; American Idol 美国偶像; Britain's Got Talent 英国达人

美国各大主要媒体

ABC 美国广播公司; NBC 全国广播公司; CBS 美国哥伦比亚广播公司; CNN 有线电视新闻网; FOX 美国福克斯广播公司; The New York Times《纽约时报》; Chicago Tribune《芝加哥论坛报》

英国各大主要媒体

Reuters 路透社；The Sun《太阳报》；The Financial Times《金融时报》；BBC 英国广播公司；SKY 天空卫视；Tabloid《小报》；Mirror《镜报》；Daily Mail《每日邮报》

奥斯卡金像奖

Best Motion Picture 最佳影片；Best Director 最佳导演；Best (Leading) Actor 最佳男主角；Best (Leading) Actress 最佳女主角；Best Supporting Actor 最佳男配角；Best Supporting Actress 最佳女配角；Best Foreign Film 最佳外语片；Best Arts/Set Direction 最佳艺术指导；Best Cinematography 最佳摄影；Best Costume Design 最佳服装设计；Best Visual Effects 最佳视觉特效

世界500强

Wal-Mart Stores 沃尔玛；BP 英国石油公司；Sinopec Group 中国石油化工集团公司；State Grid 国家电网公司；Toyota Motor 丰田汽车公司；Volkswagen 大众汽车公司；Bank of America Corp. 美国银行

逝去的文化名人

Elizabeth Taylor 伊丽莎白·泰勒；Amy Winehouse 艾米·怀恩豪斯；Václav Havel 瓦茨拉夫·哈维尔；Whitney Houston 惠特尼·休斯顿；Steve Jobs 史蒂夫·乔布斯；Willy Ronis 维利·罗尼；Michael Jackson 迈克尔·杰克逊

政界名人

Barack Obama 巴拉克·奥巴马；Tony Blair 托尼·布莱尔；Nicolas Sarkozy 尼古拉斯·萨科奇；Vladimir Putin 弗拉基米罗维奇·普京；Junichiro Koizumi 小泉纯一郎；Rajiv Gandhi 拉吉夫·甘地

Unit 2

Travelling

Learning Objectives

You are able to:
- Introduce a famous tourist spot to others
- Consult a travel agency about a tour
- Make schedules for a tour
- Listen for key words and useful expressions
- Comment on package tour and backpacking
- Learn to use adverbial clause correctly
- Fill in an application form

You are suggested to:
- Recognize the English expressions related to travel, such as book a ticket or a hotel
- Be familiar with more famous tourist spots

Part I Listening and Speaking

Warm-up

Task 1

Directions: Can you figure out the English names of the famous tourist spots in the pictures? If you have difficulties, please turn to the Internet or your partner for help.

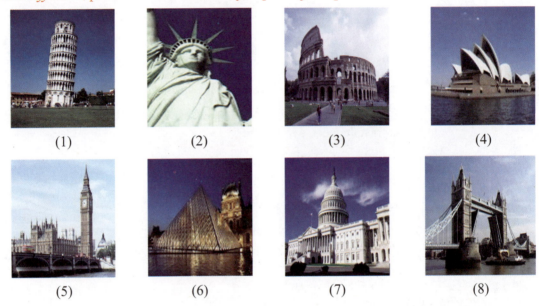

(1)　　　　　(2)　　　　　(3)　　　　　(4)

(5)　　　　　(6)　　　　　(7)　　　　　(8)

the Leaning Tower of Pisa	Big Ben	Red Square in Moscow
Tower Bridge	Pyramids	Stonehenge
the Louvre	Colosseum	Taj Mahal
White House	Sydney Opera House	the Statue of Liberty

Task 2

Directions: Can you name the following attractions in English? Work with your partner and match the Chinese words with their corresponding English expressions.

Oral Practice

Task 1

Directions: Read and practise the following dialogue with your partner, then mark the following statements with "T" or "F" according to what you have read.

Woman: Excuse me. Is this a travel agency?
Man: It is, madam. What can I do for you?
Woman: Do you have any interesting program for the two-day weekend?
Man: Oh, yes. We have lots of interesting programs for the weekend. What about St. Monica Beach? There you can swim, lie in the sun on the soft sand and play beach volleyball.
Woman: Sounds nice. What about the price?
Man: $200 each.
Woman: Good. But I will talk to my husband first. Thank you!
Man: You're welcome.

_____ 1. The woman needs some information about a trip for the weekend.
_____ 2. The travel agency has lots of good weekend programs for the customers.
_____ 3. The woman seems to have more to say in the family.

Task 2

Directions: Use the information given below to create a role-play.

National Day is approaching. Your group wants to go on a tour together. Work in groups and arrange a group tour schedule of scenic spots in your area.

Listening Practice

Task 1

Directions: Now you will hear five short conversations. They will be read only once. After each conversation, there is a question. Listen carefully and choose the best answer from the four choices.

1. ☐ To travel. ☐ To work. ☐ To study. ☐ To meet friends.
2. ☐ He is glad to take the guests to the airport.
   ☐ He has to get his car in the garage first.
   ☐ The woman should try someone else.
   ☐ He has to repair his car first.
3. ☐ She received her passport last week.
   ☐ She plans to stay in South America for a month.
   ☐ She still hasn't received her passport yet.
   ☐ She will leave for South America in a week.
4. ☐ 7:30. ☐ 8:10. ☐ 7:40. ☐ 10:00.
5. ☐ To the museum. ☐ To a wedding. ☐ To India. ☐ To an art school.

Task 2

Directions: Now you will hear a long conversation. It will be read twice. Then you are required to answer the following questions by making correct choices.

1. When will Diana's vacation start?
   ☐ In a few days' time. ☐ In two weeks' time.
2. Where is Diana going to stay while she's on vacation?
   ☐ In a luxurious hotel near the beach. ☐ With her friends.
3. Where is Ken going to have his vacation?
   ☐ At the beach, too. ☐ He has not thought about it yet.

Task 3

Directions: Now you will hear a short passage. It will be read three times. Then you are required to put in the missing information.

    Venice is the "Queen of the Adriatic Sea". Every year _____ from all over the world _____ to Italy to visit the city. Do you know why they like to go there for a visit?

    Venice is a very beautiful city. It is quite _____ from other cities in the world. There aren't any _____ in the city, so there aren't any cars or buses. There are many canals in the city. There is one big canal and _____ small canals. People move up and down the canals in boats to go to work, _____ or visit their friends.

Unit 2 Travelling

New Words and Expressions

agency	/ˈeɪdʒənsɪ/	n.	代理,代理处,政府机构
reservation	/rezəˈveɪʃn/	n.	预订
vacation	/vəˈkeɪʃn/	n.	休假,假期
garage	/ˈgærɑːʒ/	n.	车库;汽车修理行
canal	/kəˈnæl/	n.	运河,沟渠

Las Vegas

A city in the State of Nevada, U.S.A., famous for its many gambling casinos, night clubs and big hotels. The city has become a major tourist attraction in the United States.

St. Monica Beach

A beach in Los Angeles, U.S.A., an ideal tourist spot for relaxation on the western coast of America.

Part II Reading

Text A

Before Reading:

1. Are you familiar with the following pictures? What are they? Have you ever been to some well-known places? How do you feel about them?

(1)　　　　(2)　　　　(3)　　　　(4)

(5)　　　　(6)　　　　(7)　　　　(8)

2. Do you like package tour (跟团旅行) or backpacking (背包旅行)? Give your reasons.
3. While backpacking, what do you intend to bring with you?

Backpacking and Youth Hostels

Backpacking refers to a form of low-cost, independent international travel. They are also called "independent travel" or "budget travel". The lifestyle of backpacking became popular in the 2000s, when many low-cost airlines and cheap accommodations appeared. Digital communication also made backpacking much easier than before.

Backpackers are typically young adults who carry backpacks or other convenient luggage, and travel long distances or for long periods of time. Some university students backpack in their gap year. Many young people think of backpacking as a way of education instead of a vacation. Their purposes of travelling include meeting local people, seeing famous sights, and learning about different cultures.

Backpackers usually use public transport and live in youth hostels during their trip. Youth hostels provide cheap accommodation where backpackers can meet many young friends from all over the world. A guest can rent a bunk bed in a dormitory room and share the bathroom and the kitchen with other guests. Some rooms are single-sex, but others are mixed. Some hostels may also have a small number of single rooms. Sometimes, the hostel employs some long-term residents as clerks or housekeepers, and offers them free accommodation in return.

There are several differences between hostels and hotels, including:

1. Hostels are much cheaper than hotels. Young people choose hostels because they have less money to spend and lower requirement for comfort. Many hostels today, however, have improved their living conditions. Some hostels hold interesting activities to share books, DVDs, and other items among their guests.

2. Hostels are more informal than hotels. For example, hostels seldom provide food as hotels do.

3. There is less privacy in a hostel than

a hotel. But hostels have more common areas, and the rooms are usually dormitories. Therefore, there are more opportunities for the guests to socialize.

4. Hostels provide more adventurous travel than hotels. As a result, young people, especially backpackers, prefer hostels to hotels.

Hostels also have problems. For example, since guests may share a common living space, some people may steal others' belongings. Many hostels use security methods to prevent theft. One of these methods is giving a private locker to every guest. Other safety measures of the hostels include 24-hour security and CCTV. Another problem is sleeping difficulty due to noise made by other guests, such as snoring or returning late in the evening. Experienced backpackers would bring a pair of earplugs with them to solve this problem on their trips.

New Words

（标★为A级词汇，标☆为超纲词汇）

backpacking	/ˈbækˌpækɪŋ/	n.	背包旅行
hostel	/ˈhɒstl/	n.	青年招待所
refer	/rɪˈfɜː/	v.	指，归因于……
independent	/ˌɪndɪˈpendənt/	adj.	自食其力的，自力更生的
★budget	/ˈbʌdʒɪt/	adj.	低价的，低廉的
lifestyle	/ˈlaɪfstaɪl/	n.	生活方式
airline	/ˈeəlaɪn/	n.	[常用复数]航空公司
★accommodation	/əˌkɒməˈdeɪʃn/	n.	住处，住所
backpacker	/ˈbækpækə/	n.	背着背包徒步旅行者
typically	/ˈtɪpɪklɪ/	adv.	通常，一般
convenient	/kənˈviːnɪənt/	adj.	方便的，便利的
luggage	/ˈlʌɡɪdʒ/	n.	行李
purpose	/ˈpɜːpəs/	n.	目的，用途；意志
sight	/saɪt/	n.	[复数]值得一看的东西；风景，名胜
transport	/ˈtrænspɔːt/	n.	交通工具，运输工具
★dormitory	/ˈdɔːmɪtrɪ/	n.	宿舍，集体寝室
mixed	/mɪkst/	adj.	男女合住的
long-term	/lɒŋˈtɜːm/	adj.	长期的
★resident	/ˈrezɪdənt/	n.	居民；住户；居住者
housekeeper	/ˈhaʊsˌkiːpə/	n.	办公室（或房屋）管理员
activity	/ækˈtɪvətɪ/	n.	活动
item	/ˈaɪtəm/	n.	条，条款；项，项目；条目
privacy	/ˈprɪvəsɪ; ˈpraɪvəsɪ/	n.	隐私；独处；清静
socialize	/ˈsəʊʃəˌlaɪz/	v.	进行社交活动；与人交往

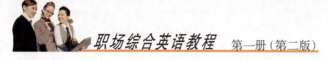

☆adventurous	/ədˈventʃərəs/	adj.	勇于冒险的；敢于创新的；新奇的
★security	/sɪˈkjuərəti/	n.	防卫；保安措施；安全工作
theft	/θeft/	n.	偷窃，盗窃
☆locker	/ˈlɒkə/	n.	寄物柜，储物柜
measure	/ˈmeʒə/	n.	[常作复数]措施，办法；步骤
snore	/snɔː/	v.	打鼾，打呼噜
experienced	/ɪkˈspɪərɪənst/	adj.	有经验的，经验丰富的
earplug	/ˈɪəplʌɡ/	n.	耳塞

Phrases and Expressions

refer to sb/sth	涉及；与……相关
gap year	空档年，间隔年
think of sb/sth as sb/sth	把……看作；把……视为
instead of	代替；作为……的替换
bunk bed	双层床铺
in return	作为回报；作为……的报酬；作为交换
as a result	结果
due to	[口语]因为，由于

Proper Names

CCTV	闭路电视

Exercises

I. Reading Comprehension

Directions: Answer the questions or complete the statements by choosing A, B, C, or D according to the text.

1. What leads to the popularity of backpacking?
   A. Digital communication.
   B. Low-cost airlines and cheap accommodations.
   C. More leisure time.
   D. Both A and B.
2. The following are the purposes of backpacking for many young people EXCEPT _____.
   A. a way of education
   B. taking a vacation
   C. meeting local people and seeing famous sights
   D. learning about different cultures
3. Which of the following is NOT MENTIONED as the difference between hostels and hotels?
   A. Hotels are usually larger than hostels.
   B. Hostels are cheaper and more informal than hotels.
   C. Hostels provide more adventurous travel than hotels.
   D. There is less privacy in a hostel than a hotel.
4. Why do young people, especially backpackers, prefer hostels to hotels?
   A. Because hostels are more informal than hotels.
   B. Because there are more opportunities for young people to socialize.
   C. Because hostels provide more adventurous travel than hotels.
   D. Because there is less privacy in a hostel than a hotel.
5. What are the problems of Youth Hostels?
   A. No privacy.
   B. No food supply or water.
   C. Terrible living conditions.
   D. Theft and sleeping difficulty.

II. Identifying Pictures

Directions: Are you familiar with the places of interest in the following pictures? Have you ever been there? What other tourist attractions in our country have you been to?

(1)

(2)

(3)

(4)

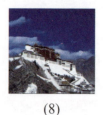

　　　　(5)　　　　　　　　(6)　　　　　　　　(7)　　　　　　　　(8)

III. Blank Filling

Directions: Use the following words or expressions in the box to translate parts of the following sentences.

| refer to | due to | instead of | in return | purpose |
| socialize | convenient | measure | think of | learn about |

1. His passion for her made him unhappy, because _____（她没有回报他的爱）.
2. When I said some people are stupid, I was _____（不是指你）.
3. _____（本次讨论的真正目的）is not to tell parents how much or how little to give to their children.
4. The restaurant's success was _____（是因为它的新经理）.
5. People do not _____（和邻居们交往）as much as they used to.
6. Whether you plan to stay for a week or for a year in a new place, you will benefit from _____（去之前了解一些当地情况）.
7. We must _____（安排一个方便的时间和地点）for the meeting.
8. _____（看一个人的手指而不是他的钱包）can let you know whether he is rich, a new study suggests.
9. He was a man who _____（除了生意对什么都不关心的人）.
10. The doctors _____（已经采取措施）to prevent cancer from developing.

IV. True or False

Directions: Tell whether the following statements are true or false. Write "T" if the statement is true and "F" if it is false.

_____ 1. Backpackers are usually young adults, including university students in their gap year.

_____ 2. Backpackers usually use public transport and live in hotels during their trip.

_____ 3. There are only single-sex rooms in youth hostels.

_____ 4. Hostels do not provide guests with food.

_____ 5. To prevent theft, all the hostels give a private locker to every guest.

Text B

Before Reading:

1. How did you feel when you graduated from high school? And what did you do in the period after you finished high school and before you went to college?
2. What is Gap Year? And what do you think of the practice of Gap Year?

Gap Year

Gap year refers to a period of time in which students go away from formal education and participate in other activities, such as travel or work. People also call it in other names, too, including time-off and time-out. Many young people take their gap year after they finish high school and before they go to university. The length of gap year is 12 months for many students, but they are also allowed to go away for shorter or longer time.

History of Gap Year

The practice of taking a gap year first appeared in the United Kingdom in the

1960s. At that time, many students went travelling, took part in volunteer work in other countries, or participated in a working holiday abroad.

In the United States, the gap year idea grew popular in the 1980s. Since then, students in many other countries, including Australia, New Zealand, and Canada, began to take their time-off. Many of these students took part in international education programs that might combine language study, home-stays, cultural communication, community service, and independent study.

In the year 2010, the practice of gap year increased among graduates from high schools, colleges, and universities. Many young adults thought that gap year experience was a good choice for their future career development. In the year 2011, however, the number of students from the UK who took time-out declined. According to researchers, there were two reasons for this trend: first, courses are more difficult to study, and students were afraid that they might not be able to catch up with their classmates after they returned; second, the university fees kept increasing, and students did not want to wait one more year before they entered college, which might be more expensive than the current price.

Gap Year Practices in Different Countries

1. The United States

In the past, fewer students from the United States take a year-off than countries like the UK, Australia, and New Zealand. Recently, however, gap year has become more popular for American students, because they feel exhausted from their high school education and want to understand themselves better outside the classroom. Many famous universities, including Harvard, Princeton, and MIT, have formal policies allowing students to delay their start of university life. It is interesting that many 21-23 year-old Americans like to take their gap year after they graduate from university.

2. Australia

Australia is a popular destination for overseas gap year travelers. On the other

hand, it is also common for Australian students to travel during their gap year. Usually, around 2% of Australians take a year off before they enter university, and travel backpacking abroad or within Australia.

New Words

标★为A级词汇，标☆为超纲词汇

formal	/ˈfɔːml/	adj.	正规的，正式的
participate	/pɑːˈtɪsɪpeɪt/	v.	参与，参加
☆time-off		n.	补假
☆time-out		n.	休息时间，暂停
length	/leŋθ/	n.	时间的长短
volunteer	/ˌvɒlənˈtɪə/	n.	志愿者，自愿参加者，志愿从事者
abroad	/əˈbrɔːd/	adv.	在国外；到海外
program	/ˈprəʊɡræm/	n.	程序；计划；大纲
☆home-stay	/ˈhəʊmsteɪ/	n.	寄宿家庭（指和房东住在一起，由房东提供食宿）
community	/kəˈmjuːnətɪ/	n.	社区；社会；乡镇；公社
increase	/ɪnˈkriːs/	v.	增加，增大，增多
adult	/ˈædʌlt, əˈdʌlt/	n.	成年人
decline	/dɪˈklaɪn/	v.	下降，减少
researcher	/rɪˈsɜːtʃə/	n.	研究员
trend	/trend/	n.	倾向，趋势，动向
fee	/fiː/	n.	费用
recently	/ˈriːsntlɪ/	adv.	最近地
★exhausted	/ɪɡˈzɔːstɪd/	adj.	精疲力竭的，疲惫不堪的，非常疲乏的
policy	/ˈpɒləsɪ/	n.	政策，原则
delay	/dɪˈleɪ/	v.	延迟，延期
★destination	/ˌdestɪˈneɪʃn/	n.	终点，目的地
overseas	/ˌəʊvəˈsiːz/	adj.	海外的，国外的

Phrases and Expressions

catch up with	追上，赶上，跟上
on the other hand	另一方面

Proper Names

Harvard	哈佛大学
Princeton	普林斯顿大学
MIT	麻省理工学院

Exercises

I. Summary

Directions: Fill in the blanks with the appropriate words according to your understanding.

    Gap year refers to (1) _____ in which students go away from (2) _____ and participate in (3) _____, such as travel or work. Many young people take their gap year after they finish (4) _____ and before they (5) _____. The (6) _____ of gap year is 12 months for many students, but they are also allowed to go away for shorter or longer time.

    The (7) _____ of taking a gap year first appeared in the (8) _____ in the 1960s. In the United States, the gap year idea grew popular (9) _____. Since then, students in many other countries, including Australia, New Zealand, and Canada, began to take their (10) _____.

II. Comprehension Based on the Text

Directions: Complete the following two statements based on the text.

1. Recently, gap year has become more popular for American students, because they _____ from their high school education and want to understand themselves better outside the classroom.
2. Usually, around 2% of Australians _____ before they enter university, and travel backpacking abroad or within Australia.

III. Vocabulary & Structures

Directions: Choose the proper words or expressions in the box and fill in the blanks.

participate in	exhausted	trend	decline
volunteer	combine	delay	catch up with
destination	on the other hand		

1. Our technology is more advanced, but other countries are _____ us.
2. The movie lost money; reviews, _____, were very favorable.
3. Everyone in the class is expected to _____ these discussions.
4. Car sales have _____ by a quarter.
5. You look absolutely _____.
6. Most of the relief work was done by _____.
7. The current _____ is towards more part-time employment.

8. Due to the fog, the plane arrived at the _____ an hour late.
9. Diets are most effective when _____ with exercise.
10. Big companies often _____ paying their bills.

IV. Translation

Directions: Put the following English sentences into Chinese.

1. Gap year refers to a period of time in which students go away from formal education and participate in other activities, such as travel or work.
2. Many young people take their gap year after they finish high school and before they go to university.
3. Young people choose hostels because they have less money to spend and lower requirement for comfort.
4. Many young adults thought that gap year experience was a good choice for their future career development.
5. Another problem is sleeping difficulty due to noise made by other guests, such as snoring or returning late in the evening.

Part III Grammar Review

状语从句

状语从句在句中作状语，状语从句由从属连词引导，根据其作用分为时间状语从句、地点状语从句、原因状语从句、条件状语从句、让步状语从句、方式状语从句、比较状语从句、目的状语从句和结果状语从句等。

1. 时间状语从句

引导时间状语从句的连接词包括：when, after, before, as soon as, while, as , the moment (that), since, whenever, hardly...when, no sooner...than, by the time 等。如：

Hardly had I opened the door when my cell phone rang.
刚打开门，我的手机就响了。
I'll let you know as soon as it is arranged.
等一安排好我就通知你。
Tell me the moment (that) you get the results.
你一拿到结果就给我打电话。

2. 地点状语从句

引导地点状语从句的连接词主要是 where 和 wherever。如：
Wherever there is plenty of sun and rain, the fields are green.
凡是阳光和雨水充足的田地，都是绿油油的。

Wuhan lies where the Yangtze and the Han River meet.
武汉位于长江和汉水汇合处。

3. 原因状语从句

引导原因状语从句的连接词主要包括：as, because, since, in that, now that, considering that, seeing that 等。如：

He had to stay in bed because he was caught in the rain and had a bad cold.
他必须待在床上，因为他淋雨得了重感冒。

As he wasn't ready in time, we went without him.
由于他未及时准备好，我们没等他就走了。

Since no one is against it, we will adopt the suggestion.
既然没有人反对这个建议，我们将采纳它。

They did the job quite well, considering that they had no experience.
考虑到他们没有什么经验，但他们干得还是不错的。

4. 让步状语从句

引导让步状语从句的连接词包括：although, though, however, whatever, whoever, whomever, whichever, whenever, wherever, whether, no matter (who, what, etc.), even if, even though, while（虽然；然而）等。如：

Although it's raining, they are still working in the field.
虽然在下雨，但他们仍在地里干活。

Don't lose confidence whatever you do.
不管你做什么，都不要失去信心。

We'll go hiking even if/ though the weather is bad.
即使天气不好，我们也要去远足。

5. 结果状语从句

引导结果状语从句的连接词包括：so (that), so...that, such that, such...that 等。如：

The wind was so strong that we could hardly move forward.
风刮得那么大，我们简直寸步难行。

Jenny is such a considerate girl that all of us like her very much.
詹妮是如此体贴的女孩，我们都非常喜欢她。

6. 方式状语从句

引导方式状语从句的连接词包括：as, as if, as though 等。如：

Air is to man as water is to fish.
空气对于人就像水对于鱼一样。

Do in Rome as the Romans do. 入乡随俗。

They talked loudly as if nobody were around.
他们大声说话仿佛周围没人似的。

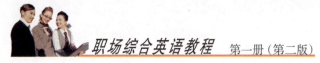

7. 比较状语从句

引导比较状语从句的连接词包括as...as, not as/so...as, than, the+比较级等。如：

Jack is as tall as Bob. 杰克和汤姆一样高。

The more he thought about it, the angrier he grew. 他越想越生气。

8. 条件状语从句

引导条件状语从句的连接词包括：if, so long as, unless, providing/provided, only if, once, suppose/supposing, on condition that等。如：

He won't lend you his car unless you promise him that you will be careful.

除非你保证小心仔细,否则他不会将汽车借给你。

You may use my dictionary as long as you don't keep it too long.

只要使用时间不太长,你可以用我的词典。

Tell me in case you get into difficulty. 遇到困难请告诉我。

I will come on condition (that) she is invited too. 如果邀请她来,那我就来。

9. 目的状语从句

引导目的状语从句的从属连词包括：so that, in order that, lest, for fear that, in case等。目的状语从句中一般含有can, could, may, might, will, would 等情态动词。如：

He spoke in a loud voice in order that every one of us could hear him.

他大声说话以便我们都能听得到。

I hid the key for fear that/in case/lest she should see it.

我把钥匙藏了起来,以防被她看见。

Assignment 1

Directions: There are ten incomplete statements here. You are required to complete each statement by choosing the appropriate answer from the four choices marked A, B, C, and D.

1. _____ difficult the task may be, we will try our best to complete it in time.
   A. No matter   B. No wonder   C. Though   D. However

2. _____ the day went on, the weather got worse.
   A. With   B. Since   C. While   D. As

3. Father was _____ busy in working _____ he often forgot rest or meals.
   A. very, that   B. so, that   C. such, as   D. enough, as

• Unit 2　Travelling •

4. We had hardly got to the station _____ it began to rain.
   A. until　　　　　　B. since　　　　　　C. while　　　　　　D. when
5. Helen listened carefully _____ she might discover exactly what she needed.
   A. in that　　　　　B. in order that　　　C. in case　　　　　D. even though
6. _____ no one is against it, we will adopt the proposal.
   A. While　　　　　　B. Since　　　　　　C. That　　　　　　D. For
7. It was _____ everyone went to the beach.
   A. so hot a weather that　　　　　　　　B. such hot weather
   C. a hot enough weather so that　　　　D. a very hot weather so that
8. I would like to go abroad _____ you do.
   A. as if　　　　　　B. though　　　　　　C. as　　　　　　　D. so that
9. This dress is prettier, but it costs _____ that one.
   A. twice as many as　　　　　　　　　　B. as much as twice
   C. as twice as　　　　　　　　　　　　D. twice as much as
10. Anyone can borrow books from this library _____ he keeps them clean and returns them in time.
    A. even if　　　　　B. as long as　　　　C. in order that　　　D. unless

Assignment 2

Directions: Mark out the mistakes and correct them in the blanks provided.

1. The children were running on the playground as fast as they can.

2. Since her husband had died, she had to support her family.

3. He won't go out until his mother will come.

4. He was very timid that he gave up such an easy game.

5. Tom had gone out as soon as his mother got home.

6. It was three months since he came to our school.

7. The playground of our school is larger than their school.

8. The streets in Nanjing are wider than Shanghai.

9. He brought a bottle of water with him so that he felt thirsty.

10. She sings songs as if she is a bird.

Part IV Applied Writing

Application Form（申请表）

申请表是将有关事实填写在指定的表格上，事由应表达清楚，以备查证；内容应翔实。申请表使用的范围很广，主要特点有：1.包容的信息量大，涵盖层次多；2.可以处理许多琐碎无序的信息，使之条理化、完整化；3.突出表现事物特征；4.言简意赅。

申请表的主要内容一般包括：

a. 介绍个人基本情况，如姓名、性别、籍贯、婚姻状况、身体状况、联系方式等；

b. 对所申请的内容（如学校、课程和职位等）做出具体要求，如需补充，要严格按表格要求填写。所填信息一定要详细、用词准确、表达明了；

c. 个人对所提供内容的真实性的声明和承诺；

d. 个人签名，一般应该是亲笔签名，并且名字的拼写方式和书写方式应始终保持一致；标明姓氏与护照、户口簿上的姓名相一致。

Sample 1

Application for a Visa

Family Name, Given Name, Middle Name <u>Li Lei</u>		Place of Birth (city, state, country) <u>Hefei, Anhui Province, PRC</u>
Date of Birth (month, day, year) <u>April 12th, 1990</u>	Residential Address (including apartment No. and post code) <u>Room308, Apt.3, Fangxing Rd, Hefei, Anhui Province. 230601</u>	Nationality: <u>Chinese</u>
		Sex: <u>Female</u>
Present Profession or Occupation (if retired, state past profession) _____		
What is the purpose of your trip? <u>A business visit</u>	How long will you intend to stay in the U.S.A.? <u>30 days</u>	
Marital Status Married ( ) Single (√) Widowed ( ) Divorced ( )		
Do you intend to work in the U.S.A.? Yes ( ) No (√)	Is either of your parents in the U.S.A.? Yes ( ) No (√)	
State where and approximately when you applied for a U.S. Visa? <u>Shanghai, August 1st, 2016</u>	When do you intend to depart for your stay in the U.S.A.? <u>September 1st, 2016</u>	
At what address will you reside in the U.S.A.? <u>Apt.46 Church Rd, Chicago</u>		
To which address do you wish your visa and passport sent? <u>Room308, Apt.3, Fangxing Rd, Hefei, Anhui Province. 230601</u>		

Sample 2

Job Application Form

Instructions: Print clearly in black or blue ink. Answer all questions. Sign and date the form.

PERSONAL INFORMATION:

Name _____

Street Address _____

City, State, Zip Code _____

Mobilephone Number _____

Are you eligible to work in the United States? Yes _____ No _____

If you are under age 18, do you have an employment certificate? Yes _____ No _____

POSITION/AVAILABILITY:

Position Applied for _____

Days Available: Monday _____ Tuesday _____ Wednesday _____ Thursday _____
Friday _____ Saturday _____ Sunday _____

Hours Available: from _____ to _____

What date are you available to start work? _____

EDUCATION:

Name and Address of School — Degree/Diploma — Graduation Date

_____
_____
_____

EMPLOYMENT HISTORY:

Present or Last Position:

Employer: _____

Address: _____

Supervisor: _____

Phone: _____

Email: _____

Position Title: _____

Responsibilities: _____

Salary: _____

Reason for Leaving: _____

May We Contact Your Present Employer? Yes _____ No _____

Signature _____

Date _____

◆ **申请表常用表达方式**

Family name/Any previous name/First name/Name in full/Full name
姓氏/曾用名/名字/全名

Country of citizenship/Nationality 国籍

Proposed duration of stay 计划逗留时间

Residential address (including apartment No. and postcode)
居住地址(包括公寓号和邮编)

Mailing address/Address for correspondence 通信地址

Personal details 个人详细资料

Present profession or occupation 目前职业

Marital status 婚姻状况

Assignment

Directions: This part is to test your ability to do practical writing. Suppose you are going to apply for IELTS. Please fill in the application form with the information given in Chinese.

按照下面信息填写一份申请表：

　　胡佳，女，1991年5月2号生于合肥。家庭住址：安徽省合肥市芜湖路123号。邮政编码：232321。电子邮件地址：Jiahu1991@126.com。现准备去英国留学。其他内容自拟。

IELTS
Application form

① Last (family) name _____

② Title (Dr/Mr/Mrs/Miss/Ms) _____

③ First (given) name(s) _____

　　These names must be the same as the names on your passport/ National Identity Card.

④ Address: Please ensure the correct mailing address is given, since your results will be sent to this address.
_____

⑤ Telephone/ Mobile number _____

⑥ Email _____

⑦ Date of birth (d/m/y) _____ ⑧ Gender F M (circle as appropriate)

⑨ Which country are you applying to go to?
　　☐ Australia   ☐ Canada   ☐ New Zealand   ☐ The United Kingdom
　　☐ The United States of America   ☐ other, please specify _____

⑩ Which IELTS test model are you taking?
　　☐ Academic   ☐ General Training

Part V Cultural Express

Round-the-world Airline Ticket

A round-the-world airline ticket is also known as RTW ticket. It is a product that enables travelers to fly around the world at a very low cost. In the past, travelers could only buy RTW tickets from a small number of airlines. Now, RTW tickets are offered by many airline groups and some travel agencies. Many travelers today buy RTW tickets when they have more time and less money to spend on their trips.

Generally, the prices of economy-class RTW tickets are from 3,000 to 5,000 USD. Some lucky travelers bought tickets for only a little more than 1,800 USD. The prices of RTW tickets differ according to travel class, origin of travel, travel distance (usually between 30,000 and 60,000 km), and sometimes season of travel. Usually, the travelers do not have to plan their trips, including the dates and journey, before they start; after they begin their trips, however, they have to pay a fee if they want to change their plan. This fee is often 100 — 150 USD, and taxes and other related fees may be added.

RTW tickets are cheap, but there are many restrictions for the travelers. Conditions for RTW tickets often include:

1. A strict limit on travel distance. Typically, the distance limits range from 26,000 to 40,000 miles, depending on the ticket price. Some RTW ticket programs do not have distance limits, but travelers are only allowed to travel to a certain number of continents.

2. A time limit. The time limit for an RTW ticket is usually 12 months after the date when the traveler started the journey.

3. A limit on number of stops. Travelers are usually required to stop no more than three times during their trip, and they may be allowed to take 5 to 16 stops depending on the ticket price. Here, an RTW stop usually refers to spending more than 24 hours in a place. Changing places in transit does not count as a stop; so many travelers use this opportunity to visit the place briefly during the day. In a small number of places, there are not many flights every day. In this case, the transit may last for several days because the travelers need to wait for the next flight to leave the place. Most travelers are happy to wait, because they can enjoy a small vacation without paying extra fees.

4. Other limits. Travelers are required to return to their starting point, or at least the country where they started the trip, as their final destination. Usually, they have to

travel in one direction only, either east or west, on each continent. This means they cannot cross the Atlantic（大西洋）or the Pacific（太平洋）more than once.

拓展词汇

机票预订

flight 航班；make a reservation 预订；reconfirm a reservation 确认预订；cancel a reservation 取消预订；change a reservation 更改预订；available 有票；travel agent 旅行社工作人员；flight schedule 航班信息；one-way ticket 单程机票；stopover 经停；business class 商务舱；first class 头等舱；window seat 靠窗座位；aisle seat 靠走道座位；departure time 出发时间；arrival time 到达时间；airport 机场

飞行安全

passenger 乘客；aircraft hijacking 劫机；check-in 登机手续；on boarding 登机；hand luggage 随身行李；bombproof 防爆的；bulletproof 防弹的；cargo hold 货舱；cockpit door 驾驶舱门；video surveillance 摄像监控；automatic guidance system 自动导航系统；air marshal 空中便衣警察

酒店预订

en suite 标间（自带卫生间的酒店房间）；double room 大床房；twin room 双床房；family room 家庭套房（包括一张大床和两张单人床）；B&B (Bed and Breakfast) 提供早餐的家庭旅店；traveler's inn 经济酒店

旅程计划

passport 护照；visa 签证；employment certification 在职证明；itinerary 行程计划；tax-free shopping 免税店购物；tax refund 退税

Unit 3

The English Language

Learning Objectives

You are able to:

☞ Talk about your experience of language learning

☞ Fulfill a questionnaire

☞ Comment on the differences between British English and American English

☞ Listen for key words and useful expressions

☞ Learn to use subject-verb agreement correctly

☞ Write a thank-you letter

You are suggested to:

☞ Understand some English expressions for daily use

☞ Be familiar with body language

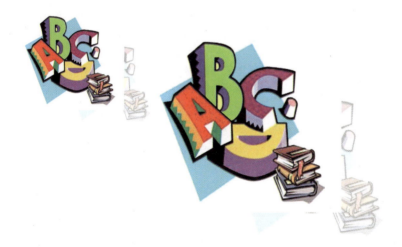

Part I Listening and Speaking

Warm-up

Task 1

Directions: Work in pairs. And fill in the blanks in the following questionnaire according to your own language learning experience.

Name _____
Sex _____
☐ What is your motivation of learning English?
_____

☐ On average, how many hours per week do you spend on English learning?
_____

☐ For you, what do you think is the biggest barrier in learning English?
_____

☐ How do you use English outside class?
_____

☐ What is the best way to ...
   learn new words and phrases?_____
   improve pronunciation?_____
   improve listening comprehension?_____
   improve reading comprehension?_____
   improve writing skills?_____

Task 2

Directions: Have you heard of the following expressions in English? Work with your partner and match the Chinese words with their corresponding English expressions.

淡水,饮用水 ☆   ★ black stranger
化妆室 ☆   ★ French chalk
图谋害人的礼物 ☆   ★ confidence man
新手 ☆   ★ pull one's leg
常识 ☆   ★ sweet water
滑石粉 ☆   ★ green hand
红茶 ☆   ★ dressing room
完全陌生的人 ☆   ★ Greek gift
开玩笑 ☆   ★ black tea
骗子,诈欺者 ☆   ★ horse sense

46

• Unit 3　The English Language •

Oral Practice

Task 1

Directions: Read and practise the following dialogue with your partner, then mark the following statements with "T" or "F" according to what you have read.

(Miss Ma is a reporter with a local newspaper. She is now interviewing a student on campus.)

Ma: Excuse me, do you speak English?
Student: Yes.
Ma: Ok, I'd like to ask you a few questions about how you learn English, and what problems you have in learning English.
Student: All right.
Ma: How long have you been learning English?
Student: Oh, for about six years, I think.
Ma: When did you begin to learn English?
Student: When I was in elementary school.
Ma: What is the biggest problem you have in learning English?
Student: Memorizing words. I find it difficult to spell English words correctly.
Ma: Well, English words are difficult to spell, even for native speakers. Now what other problems do you have in learning English?
Student: Listening and speaking English. I cannot speak English very well.
Ma: Actually, your English is good, I mean it.
Student: Oh, thank you.
Ma: Another question. Do you speak English every day?
Student: No, I don't speak English every day. I speak English only when I have English classes. But I try to read English every day if I have time.
Ma: All right. That's all for our interview. And thank you very much.
Student: You are welcome. Bye.
Ma: Bye-bye.

_____ 1. Miss Ma would like to write an article about English learning for a local newspaper.
_____ 2. The biggest problem the student has in learning English is listening and speaking.
_____ 3. The student speaks English every day to improve his spoken English.

Task 2

Directions: Use the information given below to create a role-play.

Instead of using words, we can express ourselves in many other ways, such as body language. Please look at the pictures below. What do these gestures mean? Suppose you are a native speaker, try to explain the meanings of these gestures to your partner.

(1) Thumbs up

(2) "V" gesture

(3) "OK" gesture

(4) Finger quote-mark gesture

(5) Crossed fingers

Listening Practice

Task 1

Directions: Now you will hear five short conversations. They will be read only once. After each conversation, there is a question. Listen carefully and choose the best answer from the four choices.

1. ☐ French ☐ Chinese
   ☐ Japanese ☐ English
2. ☐ For half a year. ☐ For two and a half years.
   ☐ For six years and a half. ☐ For six years.
3. ☐ The woman didn't get the job. ☐ God would help the woman.
   ☐ The woman got the job. ☐ The man would help the woman.
4. ☐ Because he has no time to study. ☐ Because he doesn't go to English class.
   ☐ Because he is slow. ☐ Because he hardly practices it.
5. ☐ The man doesn't like English at all.
   ☐ The man will major in biology next year.
   ☐ The man does well in English.
   ☐ The man likes English but does poorly in it.

Unit 3 The English Language

Task 2

Directions: Now you will hear a long conversation. It will be read twice. Then you are required to answer the following questions by making correct choices.

1. What language is the woman studying in the college?
   ☐ East Asian languages ☐ Japanese
2. What does the woman think about the language?
   ☐ It's difficult but interesting. ☐ It's very useful.
3. What does the woman do to improve her language?
   ☐ She speaks the language as much as possible.
   ☐ She reads a lot about the country.
4. What does the man say about language learning?
   ☐ Understanding culture helps language learning.
   ☐ To learn a language well requires a lot of practice.

Task 3

Directions: Now you will hear a short passage. It will be read three times. Then you are required to put in the missing information.

There are thousands of languages in the world. And English is one of the world's most _____ used languages. People use a language _____: as a native language, as a second language, or as a _____ language. English is spoken as a native language by nearly _____ people: in the United States, Britain, Australia, New Zealand, Canada, some Caribbean countries, and South Africa. As a second language, English is often necessary for official business, _____, information and other activities in a great many countries such as India, Pakistan, Nigeria, Singapore, and the Philippines. It is one of the few "working" languages of the _____ and is more frequently used than the others.

New Words and Expressions

elementary	/ˌelɪˈmentrɪ/	adj.	基本的, 初级的, 基础的, 小学的
Australia	/ɒˈstreɪlɪə/	n.	澳洲; 澳大利亚
New Zealand	/njuːˈziːlənd/	n.	新西兰
Caribbean	/ˌkærɪˈbiːən/	n.	加勒比海
		adj.	加勒比海的, 加勒比族的
Pakistan	/ˌpɑːkɪˈstɑːn/	n.	巴基斯坦
Nigeria	/naɪˈdʒɪərɪə/	n.	尼日利亚
Singapore	/ˌsɪŋəˈpɔː/	n.	新加坡
Philippine	/ˈfɪlɪpiːn/	adj.	菲律宾的, 菲律宾人的, 菲律宾群岛的
		n.	菲律宾人

Part II Reading

Text A

Before Reading:

1. There are different kinds of English, such as American English and British English in the light of the region, spoken English and written English from the perspective of using. So, in English, there are different words meaning the same things, and the same word perhaps can be pronounced quite differently.

   Now, try to give the American equivalents to the following British words. Ask your partner or consult the dictionary if necessary.

   British word: flat, underground, child, football, car, policeman, pavement, maize

2. As a language, English is actually a mixture. It consists of a lot of foreign words, especially French and Latin words. Compared with English, Chinese is much purer, but still, it contains a few words from other languages. For example, "比萨" is borrowed from the Italian word "pizza", while "考拉" is from an Aboriginal（澳洲土著人的）word "Koala". Can you list some Chinese words translated phonetically from English?

_____
_____
_____

English Is a Queer Language

Jarmila came to me with this puzzle. "Mrs. Green told me her mother is coming to visit her, and she is going to stay a week. How can she stay if she is going? How can she go if she is staying?" All I could say was a helpless "Well, it is idiomatic."

Her next question was even more difficult. Jarmila said, "Is it true that it means the same thing if you say, 'The house burned down' or 'The house burned up'? Surely if it burned up, that means the fire started from the lower part and worked up, while if it burned down, it started in the attic and worked down."

"No," I said, "it does not. You can say it either way and it means the same thing." Jarmila sighed. "I do not understand this 'up', I thought I knew the difference between up and down, but there are so many 'up's that seem quite unnecessary. Why do they tell me to hurry up when I am not going upstairs? And why must I clean up the mess, wrap up the parcel, tidy up my desk? What has 'up' to do with it all?"

Unit 3　The English Language

"Well," I began, rather helplessly, "perhaps 'clean up' seems more thorough than just 'clean'."

After a while Jarmila came back in triumph. "No," she said. "'Up' has nothing to do with thoroughness. Look now. There are three ways you can use 'make up'. I make up the bed. I make up my mind. I make up my face when I put on lipstick."

"Yes," I said, "and there is a fourth. I make up a story to please Jane."

Of course there was no explanation I could give her. You will find queer things, such as "up to now" and "it's up to you" and two "look up"s, one meaning to raise one's eyes, the other to seek information. In the end, I gave up trying to explain "up".

The next problem was a tough one. Bohus came back from work saying that if a man learned all the ways of using the word "get" he would have mastered the language. That started us on a hunt for "get", which yielded a more abundant harvest.

Just try to follow "get" down the alphabet from "get along with somebody" to "get well". Of course we get sick, too, we get ahead of somebody, get behind in our work, get homesick, get cold feet, get rich, and so on.

Even so simple an expression as "back and forth" arouses confusion, because it is illogical. "One can not go back if one does not first go forth. Why do not you say 'forth and back'?"

New Words

（标★为A级词汇，标☆为超纲词汇）

queer	/kwɪə/	adj.	古怪的
helpless	/ˈhelpləs/	adj.	无助的
puzzle	/ˈpʌzl/	n.	难题
idiomatic	/ɪdɪəˈmætɪk/	adj.	符合语言习惯的
attic	/ˈætɪk/	n.	阁楼
either	/ˈaɪðə/	pron.	（两者中）任何一个
sigh	/saɪ/	v.	叹气
unnecessary	/ʌnˈnesəsərɪ/	adj.	不必要的
mess	/mes/	n.	混乱
tidy	/ˈtaɪdɪ/	v.	整理
thorough	/ˈθʌrə/	adj.	彻底的
triumph	/ˈtraɪʌmf/	n.	胜利
thoroughness	/ˈθʌrənəs/	n.	完全，十分
lipstick	/ˈlɪpstɪk/	n.	口红
explanation	/ˌekspləˈneɪʃn/	n.	解释
tough	/tʌf/	adj.	艰苦的；艰难的
yield	/jiːld/	v.	生产，屈服
★alphabet	/ˈælfəbet/	n.	字母表

homesick	/ˈhəʊmsɪk/	adj.	想家的, 思乡的
★ arouse	/əˈraʊz/	v.	引起
☆ confusion	/kənˈfjuːʒn/	n.	困惑
★ illogical	/ɪˈlɒdʒɪkəl/	adj.	不合逻辑的
forth	/fɔːθ/	adv.	离去; 向前

Phrases and Expressions

burn down	烧毁
hurry up	赶紧
clean up	打扫
wrap up	圆满完成
have nothing to do with	与……无关
make up	组成, 编造, 化妆
up to now	到目前为止
in the end	最后, 终于
get along with	与……和睦相处
get ahead of	胜过
get cold feet	临阵退缩
back and forth	来回

Proper Names

| Jarmila | 娅米拉 |
| Bohus | 布胡斯 |

Unit 3 The English Language

Exercises

I. Reading Comprehension

Directions: Answer the questions or complete the statements by choosing A, B, C, or D according to the text.

1. It can be inferred from Jarmila's first question in Para.1 that _____.
   A. Jarmila didn't understand what Mrs. Green meant
   B. Jarmila didn't believe that Mrs. Green's mother would visit Mrs. Green and stay for a week
   C. Jarmila was too young to tell the difference between "go" and "stay"
   D. Jarmila thought it contradictory that "go" and "stay" had been used in one sentence

2. The author regards Jarmila's second question as _____.
   A. childish   B. more difficult
   C. stupid   D. unexpected

3. Which of the following statements is not true according to the passage?
   A. Jarmila thought that there were so many "up"s that seemed quite unnecessary in English.
   B. The author failed to give any explanation to Jarmila regarding the different usage of "up".
   C. They found that they could learn more from the hunt for "up" than for "get".
   D. The author thought that "back and forth" aroused confusion because it is illogical.

4. What does Bohus most probably imply by saying "if a man learned all the ways of using the word 'get' he would have mastered the language"?
   A. The word "get" has been very widely and frequently used in English.
   B. It's unnecessary for a man to learn any other word in English except "get".
   C. English is not so difficult a language as people think.
   D. It's impossible for a man to learn all the ways of using the word "get".

5. In the author's opinion, English is queer because _____.
   A. some usages of English are contradictory in particular contexts
   B. some expressions are so illogical that people feel confused easily
   C. it's very hard to explain many idiomatic expressions
   D. all mentioned above

II. Vocabulary

Directions: Complete each of the following sentences with the correct form of the italicized words given in the brackets.

1. Elizabeth was staring at her daughter with a _____ *(puzzle)* frown.
2. John stood there and repeated her name _____ *(helpless)*.
3. She says it is hard to _____ *(explanation)* in detail how the drug appears to work.
4. _____ *(general)* speaking, table manners vary from culture to culture.
5. My words surprised and _____ *(confusion)* him.

6. I really enjoy _____ *(work)* together with you, and thank you for your cooperation.
7. We will set up a factory in that country, which is rich in _____ *(nature)* resources.
8. I'll not be able to attend the conference unless somebody pays my _____ *(expensive)*.
9. They have already discussed the report _____ *(give)* by the department manager.
10. My first _____ *(impress)* of England was that it was a grey and rainy place.

III. Blank Filling

Directions: Use the phrases in the box to translate parts of the following sentences.

clean up	back and forth	hurry up	get along with
get ahead of	in the end	up to now	make up
look up	have nothing to do with		

1. It's a bit difficult to _____ (与不喜欢的人相处).
2. He always tries to _____ (超过别人) in everything.
3. George used to _____ (在院子里来回踱步) when he felt tired.
4. I planned to pay a visit to that mysterious village, but _____ (最终还是没去).
5. Tom said he _____ (与那事件毫无关系).
6. He _____ (习惯于编造借口) about his father being ill.
7. Can you _____ (查一查下个航班的时间)?
8. _____ (到目前为止) I always thought Smith was honest.
9. Franklin told Mary to _____ (快点洗澡); otherwise, they'd miss their train.
10. It's your turn to _____ (打扫教室).

IV. True or False

Directions: Tell whether the following statements are true or false. Write "T" if the statement is true and "F" if it is false.

_____ 1. When Jarmila came to the author with her puzzle, all he could say was a helpless "Well, it is idiomatic".
_____ 2. Jarmila found that there were three ways of using the phrase "make up".
_____ 3. What Bohus said after his coming back from work started us on a hunt for "get".
_____ 4. According to the author, it is easy for us to understand "back and forth" because it is logical.
_____ 5. It can be inferred from the text that English is queer because there are too many idiomatic expressions in it.

Text B

Before Reading:

1. Do you agree that the English history has had a profound influence on the English language? Why or why not?

2. In comparison, which language do you think has a larger vocabulary, English or Chinese? Many people insist that the main problem for them to improve their English is that they can not very easily memorize new words. What's your proposal for overcoming this difficulty?

The Glorious Messiness of English

The story of our English language is typically one of massive stealing from other languages. That is why English today has a vocabulary of over one million words, while other major languages have far fewer. How did the language of a small island become the language of the planet — more widely spoken and written than any other has ever been?

When Caesar invaded Britain in 55 B.C., English did not exist. The Celts who had been living there spoke languages that survive today as Welsh, Gaelic and Breton.

English came into existence when Germanic tribes went across the North Sea to settle in Britain. Most scholars agree that the Jutes and the Saxons migrated to the south of Britain, and the Angles settled in the north and east. Together they formed what we call Anglo-Saxon society.

The Anglo-Saxons passed on to us their farming vocabulary, including sheep, shepherd, ox, earth, wood, field and work. They must have also enjoyed themselves because they gave us the words glee, laughter and mirth.

The big influence on English was first due to Christianity. Wanting to bring the faith to the Angles, Pope Gregory I. sent monks who built churches. This enriched the Anglo-Saxon vocabulary with some 400 to 500 words from Greek and Latin, such as angel.

Later in history, into this relatively peaceful land came the Vikings from Scandinavia. They also brought to English many words that begin with *sk*; like *sky* and *skirt*.

Another flood of new vocabulary occurred in 1066, when the Normans conquered England. The country now had three languages: French for the aristocrats, Latin for the churches and English for the common people. In everyday life the Normans ate *beef*, while the English ate *ox* or *cow*.

Around 1476 William Caxton set up a printing workshop in England and started a communications revolution. Printing brought into English the wealth of new thinking. Translations of Greek and Roman works were poured onto the printed page, and with them were thousands of Latin words like *capsule* and *habitual*, and Greek words like *catastrophe* and *thermometer*.

With the development of scientific revolution, words like *atmosphere* and

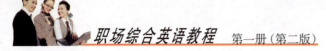

skeleton had been created. Today we still borrow from Latin and Greek to name new inventions, like *video*, *television* and *cyberspace*.

Indeed, English is the tongue of the common man. Think of how many English words have come from poker players, cowboys and jazz musicians. Now new words are even coming from computer hackers and rap artists. Some words may be thought beautiful and some ugly; some may live and some may die. But it is all English, and it has always belonged to everyone.

New Words

（标★为A级词汇，标☆为超纲词汇）

glorious	/ˈglɔːrɪəs/	adj.	辉煌的
messiness	/ˈmesɪnəs/	n.	杂乱状况
massive	/ˈmæsɪv/	adj.	大量的
major	/ˈmeɪdʒə/	adj.	主要的
★invade	/ɪnˈveɪd/	v.	侵略
exist	/ɪɡˈzɪst/	v.	存在
survive	/səˈvaɪv/	v.	幸存
migrate	/maɪˈɡreɪt/	v.	迁移
form	/fɔːm/	v.	组成
shepherd	/ˈʃepəd/	n.	牧羊人
★ox	/ɒks/	n.	公牛
☆glee	/gliː/	n.	快乐
☆mirth	/mɜːθ/	n.	欢乐, 欢笑
Christianity	/ˌkrɪstɪˈænətɪ/	n.	基督教
faith	/feɪθ/	n.	信念
monk	/mʌŋk/	n.	僧侣
conquer	/ˈkɒŋkə/	v.	征服
☆aristocrat	/ˈærɪstəkræt/	n.	贵族
workshop	/ˈwɜːkʃɒp/	n.	工场; 作坊
wealth	/welθ/	n.	财富
pour	/pɔː/	v.	涌出
☆capsule	/ˈkæpsjuːl/	n.	航天舱
catastrophe	/kəˈtæstrəfɪ/	n.	大灾难
☆thermometer	/θəˈmɒmɪtə/	n.	温度计
★video	/ˈvɪdɪəʊ/	n.	录像机
cyberspace	/ˈsaɪbəˌspeɪs/	n.	信息空间
poker	/ˈpəʊkə/	n.	纸牌
cowboy	/ˈkaʊbɔɪ/	n.	牛仔
jazz	/dʒæz/	n.	爵士乐

Unit 3 The English Language

hacker	/ˈhækə/	n.	黑客
☆rap	/ræp/	n.	说唱

Phrases and Expressions

pass on to sb	转交,传给
enjoy oneself	过得快乐,玩得愉快
begin with	以……开始
a wealth of	大量,丰富
belong to	属于

Proper Names

Caesar	凯撒
Celt	凯尔特人
Welsh	威尔士语
Gaelic	盖尔语
Breton	布列塔尼语
Germanic	日耳曼人的
Jute	朱特人
Saxon	撒克逊人
Angles	盎格鲁人
Anglo-Saxon	盎格鲁撒克逊的
Pope Gregory I.	教皇格列高列一世
Viking	北欧海盗
Scandinavia	斯堪的纳维亚半岛
Norman	诺曼人
William Caxton	威廉·卡克斯顿
Roman	罗马人

Exercises

I. Summary

Directions: Fill in the blanks with the appropriate words according to your understanding.

The story of our English language is typically one of massive (1) _____ from other languages. When Caesar (2) _____ Britain in 55 B.C., English did not (3) _____ . The infusion of words came when Germanic tribes went across the North Sea to (4) _____ in Britain. The first big (5) _____ on English was from Christianity. Later, the Vikings from Scandinavia also brought to English many words. Another flood of new vocabulary (6) _____ in 1066, when the Normans conquered England. Around 1476 William Caxton set up a printing press in England and started a communications (7) _____. Printing brought into English not only the wealth of new thinking but also (8) _____ of Latin and Greek words. Indeed, English is the (9) _____ of the common man since so many words have been created by them. Now new words are even coming from computer hackers and rap artists. In a word, it is all English, and it has always (10) _____ to everyone.

II. Comprehension Based on the Text

Directions: Complete the following two statements based on the text.

1. Although English is only the language of a small island, it has become the language of the ____ _____ because no language has ever been as widely spoken and written as English.
2. Indeed, many English words have come from common man, such as poker players, cowboys and jazz musicians, etc. Now new words are even coming from _____.

III. Vocabulary & Structures

Directions: Choose the proper words or expressions in the box and fill in the blanks.

survive	get down to	glorious	pass on	a wealth of
conquer	major	enjoy oneself	exist	pour in

1. I really must _____ my studies. I have been lazy for such a long time.
2. As soon as the gate was opened, a crowd of people _____.
3. These plants can't _____ in very cold condition.
4. The late (已故的) millionaire _____ much of his fortune to his daughter.
5. The tribes were easily _____ by the Persian armies.
6. A life free from all worry just doesn't _____.
7. Their whole _____ history seemed to be reflected in the song.
8. John told his mother that the children _____ at the seaside.
9. It was not until late afternoon that Jurgis began to tackle the _____ problem.

58

10. With the deepening of economic reforms, there is _____ exciting new opportunities in China.

IV. Translation

Directions: Put the following English sentences into Chinese.

1. With the development of scientific revolution, many words had been created.
2. That is why English today has a vocabulary of over one million words, while other major languages have far fewer.
3. The story of our English language is typically one of massive stealing from other languages.
4. English came into existence when Germany tribes went across the North sea to settle in Britain.
5. Indeed, English is the tongue of the common man. Think of how many English words have come from poker players, cowboys and jazz musicians.

Part III Grammar Review

主谓一致

主谓一致指谓语动词在人称和数上与主语保持一致。按照英语语法的规定，一般情况下，句子主语为单数时，其谓语动词用单数形式；句子主语为复数时，其谓语动词用复数形式。主谓一致包括三个方面：语法一致、意义一致和就近原则。

1. 语法一致

语法一致指主语和谓语在单复数形式上的一致关系，主语为单数形式，谓语动词用单数形式；反之，谓语动词用复数形式。如：

His ambition **is** to be a musician. 他的志向是成为一名音乐家。

Reading aloud **is** very important in learning a foreign language.
学习外语时大声朗读是非常重要的。

Most leaders **were** well-educated.
大多数领导都受过良好的教育。

How they got there **doesn't** concern me. 他们怎样到达那儿与我无关。

注意：

① 由 and 或 both...and 连接两个名词或代词做主语时，谓语动词用复数形式。但如果这部分主语是具有两个身份或性质的同一人或一个完整的事物，谓语动词要用单数形式。如：

Baseball and swimming **are** usually summer sports.
棒球和游泳通常是夏季的运动。

The professor and writer **is** speaking at the meeting.
这位教授兼作家在会上发言。

② 主语前面如果有 each, every, many a, more than one, no 等修饰，谓语动词一般用单数形式。如：

Many a boy and girl **has** made the same mistake.

许多男孩和女孩都犯了同样的错误。

Every minute **and** every second is precious. 每分每秒都很珍贵。

2. 意义一致

意义一致指谓语动词在单、复数的选择上取决于主语所表达的概念，而不取决于表面上的语法标记。

① 单复数同形的词作主语，要根据意义来决定谓语动词的形式。常见名词有 fish, deer, means, sheep, species, series, works 等。如：

All possible means **have** been tried. 一切可能的方法都试过了。

Such a means **is** really unpleasant. 这样的方法确实令人不愉快。

② 集合名词作主语时谓语动词的单、复数形式要根据它们所强调的内容来定。集合名词如果表示的是整体概念，谓语动词就用单数；反之，就用复数。

The committee **was** made up of ten members. 该委员会由十个成员组成。

The committee **were** in the room. 委员们都在房间里。

③ "the+形容词（或过去分词）"作主语指一类人时，谓语动词通常用复数。

The injured **were** taken to hospital. 受伤的人都送进了医院。

The English **do** not drink much wine. 英国人不会喝很多酒。

④ 表示金钱、时间、价格、度量衡的复合名词做主语时，通常可以把这些主语看作一个整体，谓语动词一般用单数形式。

Ten dollars **is** spent on this rose.

这枝玫瑰花了十美元。

Twenty miles **is** a long distance if you have to walk.

如果你走路的话，20英里是一段很长的距离。

⑤ 形式上为复数，但意义上却是单数的名词做主语时，谓语动词用单数。如 news, Mathematics, Physics, Politics, Economics 等。

Mathematics **is** the language of science. 数学是科学语言。

His "Selected Poems" **was** first published in 1965.

他的《诗歌选集》最早是1965年出版的。

3. 就近原则

就近原则指谓语动词的数要与它紧邻的名词或代词的数保持一致。

① 由 or, either...or, neither...nor, not only...but also 连接的两个名词或代词做主语时，谓语的形式一般根据就近原则处理。如：

Either he or I **am** to go to the laboratory. 要么是他要么是我将去实验室。

Neither the students nor the teacher **knows** anything about this matter.

学生和老师都对此事一无所知。

Not only the boss but also his employees **object** to the change.
不仅是老板,连他的雇员都反对这种变化。

② 主语由 there 或 here 引导时,谓语的形式一般根据就近原则处理。如:
Here **is** a pen, a few books and some paper for you.
这儿有一支笔,几本书和一些纸给你。
There **are** fifty students and a teacher in the classroom.
教室里有50位学生和一位老师。

注意:
名词后面有 with, along with, together with, besides, except, but, like, including, as well as, rather than 等短语引出的共同主语时,谓语动词与这些短语前面的名词在单、复数形式上要保持一致。如:
All but one **were** here just now. 除了一位不在,刚才所有人都在这儿。
The teacher together with some students **is** visiting the factory.
这个老师正带着几位学生参观工厂。
Professor Rogers, as well as his students, **is** arriving tonight.
罗杰斯教授和他的学生今晚到达。

Assignment

Directions: Complete the sentences by using the words in the brackets. Pay special attention to the tense and make changes if necessary.

1. Peter, as well as his two sisters, Sondra and Emily, _____ *(are, is)* left handed.
2. A great deal of the world's coal _____ *(lie, lies)* in this country.
3. Five minutes _____ *(is, are)* too short to finish this task.
4. The young _____ *(is, are)* often very curious about the new things.
5. Two-fifths of the land in that district _____ *(is, are)* covered with trees and grass.
6. Linguistics _____ *(is, are)* a branch of study on human language.
7. Professor Taylor, with six of his students _____ *(is, are)* attending a conference in New York.
8. The police _____ *(is, are)* patrolling(巡逻)that area very carefully.
9. Neither my friends nor I _____ *(was, were)* able to persuade him to accept our advice.
10. There _____ *(is, are)* a teacher and fifty students in the classroom.

Part IV Applied Writing

Thank-you Letter（感谢信）

感谢信用于在收到礼物、问候、祝贺或受到款待、帮助时等表示感谢；在商务活动中，对于来自客户等各方面的支持、建议或服务也要表示感谢。感谢信应注意一事一谢，篇幅要简短，措辞要自然，语气要诚恳，切忌过分恭维。

感谢信的主要内容一般包括：
    a. 表达感激之情，简单陈述写这封感谢信的原因；
    b. 详细说明所要感谢的事由，措辞更加具体真诚，再次表示真挚的感谢；
    c. 向对方表达自己真诚的祝愿，再次道谢或向对方发出邀请。

Sample 1

Oct. 12, 2012

Dear Mrs. Usher,

    On behalf of the company, I would like to thank you for placing an unusually large order with us yesterday, and I want to say your continued confidence in us is very much appreciated.

    The happy working relationship between us that has lasted for many years has always been valued by us and we shall do our best to maintain it.

    Thank you once again for your kindness.

Yours sincerely,
Barbara

Sample 2

Hi John

I'm writing to thank you for those eight wonderful days in Hangzhou. I will never forget my visit.

I was a little anxious before I arrived in Hangzhou because I didn't know what to expect. But when I arrived, I knew there is no need to worry. You gave me a very warm welcome and made me feel at home very quickly. I will always remember your kindness and hospitality. And thank you, also, for arranging so many interesting activities. I know that it took a great deal of your precious time.

It was very kind of you to do so much for me and I appreciate it more than I can say.

Take care John

Danielle

◆ 感谢信常用句型

Please accept my sincere appreciation for... 请接受我对……真挚的感谢。

Thank you for taking time and trouble to... 感谢您费时费力……

Many thanks for your generous cooperation. 谢谢贵方的真诚合作。

I wish to express my profound appreciation for... 我对……深表谢意。

Thank you for your hospitality/consideration. 感谢您的盛情款待/关怀。

I hope that I may be able to return your hospitality in near future.
我希望在不久的将来能报答您的热情款待。

I am truly grateful/thankful to you for... 我真心感激您……

It was good (thoughtful) of you... 承蒙好意（关心）……

Thank you again for your wonderful hospitality and I am looking forward to seeing you soon.
再次感谢您的盛情款待，并期待不久见到您。

Assignment

Directions: This part is to test your ability to do practical writing. You are required to write a thank-you letter based on the following information given in Chinese.

假定你是 JKM 公司的 Thomas Black,刚从巴黎(Paris)出差回来,请给在巴黎的 Jane Costa 小姐写一封感谢信。

写信日期:2016 年 12 月 26 日

内容:

1. 感谢她在巴黎期间的热情接待;
2. 告诉她巴黎给你留下了美好的印象,你非常喜欢法国……参观工厂和学校后学到了很多……
3. 期待再次与她见面。

注意:必须包括对收信人的称谓、写信日期、发信人的签名等基本格式。

Part V Cultural Express

Crazy English

English is the most widely used language in the world. One in every seven human beings around the globe can speak English. And more than half of the world's books and three-quarters of international mail are written in this crazy tongue. Let's face it! English is a crazy language!

For example, there is no egg in eggplant, and you will find neither pine nor apple in a pineapple. Hamburgers are not made from ham, English muffins were not invented in England, and French fries were not invented in France.

In English, we find that quicksand can work slowly, boxing rings are square, public bathrooms have no baths, and a guinea pig is neither a pig nor is it from Guinea(几内亚). And why is it that a writer writes, but fingers do not fing, and hammers don't ham? One goose, two geese, so one moose, two meese? Tell me, if the teacher taught, why isn't it that the preacher praught? If a horsehair mat is made from the hair of horses and a camel hair coat from the hair of camels, what is the name of the animal that gives us mohair? If a vegetarian eats vegetables, what does a humanitarian eat?

In what other language do people drive on a parkway and park on a driveway? Then we recite at a play and play at a recital? And have you noticed that we have noses that run and feet that smell? How can a fat chance and a slim chance be the same thing? While a wise man and a wise guy are opposites? How can overlook and oversee be opposites, while quite a lot and quite a few are alike?

You have to marvel at the lunacy of a language in which your house can burn up as it burns down, in which you fill in a form by filling it out and in which your alarm clock goes off by going on.

English was invented by people, not by computers, and it reflects the creativity of the human race. That is why, when stars are out they are visible, but when the lights are out they are invisible. And why, when I wind up my watch I start it, but when I wind up this essay I end it.

拓展词汇

日常用语类

sleep late 起得晚（不是"睡得晚"）
think twice 三思（不是"想两次"）
busboy 餐馆勤杂工（不是"公汽售票员"）
confidence man 骗子（不是"信得过的人"）
criminal lawyer 刑事律师（不是"犯罪的律师"）
China policy 对华政策（不是"中国制定的政策"）
peace negotiation 和平谈判（不是"和平进行的谈判"）
rest room 厕所（不是"休息室"）
dressing room 化妆室（不是"试衣室"或"更衣室"）
drawing room 客厅；休息室（不是"画室"）
brown sugar 红糖（不是"棕糖"）
black tea 红茶（不是"黑茶"）
green hand 新手（不是"绿手"）
blue stocking 女学者、女才子（不是"蓝色长筒袜"）
small fortune 一大笔钱（不是"一小笔钱"）
blue film 黄色电影（不是"蓝色电影"）
late teacher 已故教师（不是"以前的教师"）
black coffee 黑咖啡（不是"浓咖啡"）

短语

eat one's words 承认说的是错的(不是"食言")
think a great deal of oneself 高看或看重自己(不是"为自己想得很多")
pull up one's socks 鼓起勇气(不是"提上袜子")
in repair 状况良好(不是"在维修中")
in good shape 身体健康(不是"体型好")

表达类

What a shame! 多可惜! 真遗憾!(不是"多可耻!")
You can say that again! 说得好!说得没错!(不是"你可以再说一遍!")
He has had it! 他吃够了苦头!(不是"他有了一个!")
I've had enough of it. 我受够了。(不是"我足够了。")
Don't let him tell you that! 别信他!(不是"别让他告诉你那件事!")
Tell me another. 我不信。(不是"告诉我另一个。")
Out of sight, out of mind. 长时间没见都忘记了。(不是"眼不见心不烦。")
I have no idea of that man. 我不了解那个人。(不是"我对那个人没意见。")

Unit 4

Online Shopping

Learning Objectives

You are able to:

☞ Talk about your online shopping experience

☞ Fulfill a questionnaire

☞ Comment on the advantages and disadvantages of online shopping

☞ Listen for key words and useful expressions

☞ Learn to use inversion correctly

☞ Write an application letter

You are suggested to:

☞ Recognize the English abbreviations which are usually used online

☞ Be familiar with some famous shopping websites

Part I Listening and Speaking

Warm-up

Task 1

Directions: Work in pairs. Ask each other questions and fill in the blanks in the following questionnaire according to your own shopping experience.

Name: _____
Sex: _____
Age: _____

1. Do you have online shopping experience?
   ☐ Yes   ☐ No
2. What online retailers do you usually use?
   ☐ Taobao   ☐ Joyo Amazon China   ☐ Dangdang
   ☐ 360 buy   ☐ Suning   Other _____
3. How do you know these online shopping websites?
   ☐ Newspaper or magazine ☐ TV commercial   ☐ Radio
   ☐ Google or Baidu   ☐ Online advertising   ☐ Friends
   Other _____
4. How often do you shop online?
   ☐ Never   ☐ Seldom   ☐ Sometimes   ☐ Always
5. How much money do you spend on online shopping each year?
   ☐ Less than 50RMB   ☐ 50—100RMB   ☐ 100—200RMB
   ☐ More than 1000RMB
6. In online shopping, what do you care about?
   ☐ Reasonable price   ☐ Good quality   ☐ Good reputation
   ☐ Good service   ☐ Effective delivery   Other _____
7. What kind of goods do you usually buy from online shopping?
   ☐ Clothes   ☐ Shoes   ☐ Bags   ☐ Books
   ☐ Electronic products   ☐ Skin care products   ☐ Cosmetic products
   Other _____
8. What do you concern about online shopping?
   ☐ Payment   ☐ Safety   ☐ Price   ☐ Quality

Task 2

Directions: Have you heard the following expressions in English? Work with your partner and match the abbreviations with their corresponding full forms.

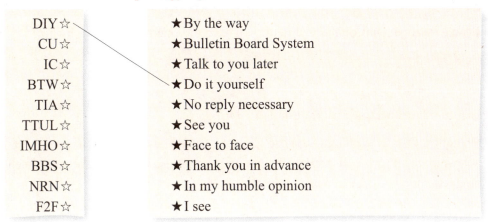

DIY ☆ — ★ Do it yourself
CU ☆ — ★ See you
IC ☆ — ★ I see
BTW ☆ — ★ By the way
TIA ☆ — ★ Thank you in advance
TTUL ☆ — ★ Talk to you later
IMHO ☆ — ★ In my humble opinion
BBS ☆ — ★ Bulletin Board System
NRN ☆ — ★ No reply necessary
F2F ☆ — ★ Face to face

Oral Practice

Task 1

Directions: Read and practice the following dialogue with your partner, then answer the questions according to what you have read.

Jennifer: That's a cool MP4 player, is it new?

Billy: No, I got it on the Internet from an exchange; someone traded me his MP4 player for my old mobile phone.

Jennifer: Really? I've heard of people buying and selling things on the Internet. I don't know people can exchange things!

Billy: Sure, as long as you find a willing partner you can swap anything. Internet exchange has just started up, but it's been developing quickly. Now there are a ton of websites and forums designed specifically for exchanging items.

Jennifer: Swapping stuff for stuff. It's really nice. We can exchange items we don't need for those you are in need of, and both benefit without wasting anything. I should get in on this too!

Billy: Well, there are some flaws about internet exchange. For example, you can't always be sure about the quality of the items you get through exchange.

Jennifer: That's right. Thank you. I will be careful.

1. What is internet exchange?
   _____

2. What does Billy worry about internet exchange?
   _____

3. Will you exchange items on the Internet if you have the chance? Why or why not?
   _____

Task 2

Directions: Use the information given below to create a role-play.

Mother's Day is coming. Suppose you are a shop assistant. Your deskmate is a customer who wants to buy a present for his or her mother. Now you are recommending some products for him or her to buy.

Suggested products: dietary supplements; comestics; clothing; bag; body-building apparatus; shoes

Listening Practice

Task 1

Directions: Now you will hear five short conversations. They will be read only once. After each conversation, there is a question. Listen carefully and choose the best answer from the four choices.

1. ☐ She doesn't like shopping online.   ☐ She has never heard of it.
   ☐ She hasn't bought anything online.   ☐ She will have a try in the future.
2. ☐ In the supermarket.   ☐ In the local department store.
   ☐ On the Internet.   ☐ In the specialty shop.
3. ☐ He thinks that they are of poor quality.
   ☐ He thinks that they are bargains.
   ☐ He thinks that they are overpriced.
   ☐ He thinks that they can be purchased at a lower price elsewhere.
4. ☐ $450.   ☐ $400.   ☐ $225.   ☐ $250.
5. ☐ She no longer likes her old cell phone.
   ☐ She lost her old cell phone.
   ☐ She lent her old cell phone to an old friend.
   ☐ She thought her cell phone was too old.

Task 2

Directions: Now you will hear a long conversation. It will be read twice. Then you are required to answer the following questions by making correct choices.

1. What will Billy and Jennifer do?
   □ Go out for a cup of tea.   □ Go shopping.
2. What do Billy and Jennifer want to buy?
   □ Onion.   □ Beef.   □ Fruit.
3. How would Billy and Jennifer like to pay?
   □ By cash.   □ By credit card.

Task 3

Directions: Now you will hear a short passage. It will be read three times. Then you are required to put in the missing information.

With only two weeks to go before Christmas, buying presents is a high priority for a lot of people. However, this year not so many people are leaving their homes to browse around the shops. These days lots of people can _____ in the comfort of their own home with the help of _____.

_____ is becoming more and more popular for a number of reasons; prices are often lower online, you don't have to _____ in busy shops and you can buy almost any product imaginable with just a few clicks of your mouse.

In the past a lot of people were reluctant to shop online. Many were _____ the security of entering their card details on the Internet and the reliability of the Internet. As shopping online has become more widespread, these worries have begun to disappear. _____ still do have security worries but it hasn't slowed down the ever-increasing numbers of online shoppers.

New Words and Expressions

exchange	/ɪksˈtʃeɪndʒ/	v.	交换, 兑换
		n.	交换, 交易所, 兑换
trade	/treɪd/	n.	贸易, 商业; 行业
		v.	贸易; 交换
swap	/swɒp/	v.	交换, 用……做交易
		n.	交换, 适合交换的东西
forum	/ˈfɔːrəm/	n.	论坛
design	/dɪˈzʌɪn/	n.	设计; 图案
		v.	设计

specifically	/spəˈsɪfɪklɪ/	adv.	特别地;明确地,具体地
stuff	/stʌf/	n.	原料,材料,东西
		v.	填满;吃饱
efficient	/ɪˈfɪʃnt/	adj.	效率高的,有能力的
flaw	/flɔː/	n.	缺点,瑕疵,缺陷
priority	/praɪˈɒrətɪ/	n.	优先(权),重点;优先考虑的事

Part II Reading

Text A

Before Reading:

1. Nowadays many people daily surf the Internet, in order to get the latest news, deal with e-mails, read and update blogs, play video games, transmit photos, or watch movies. Some of the Internet users even buy products through the Internet. Have you bought anything online? Now, please figure out the products in the pictures.

(1)   (2)   (3)   (4)   (5)

2. Do you know the advantages and disadvantages of online shopping? Please fill in the chart below with brief words:

advantages	disadvantages

Privacy and Security Issues in Online Shopping

Shopping online has never been so easy. With the increasing numbers of online merchants, people nowadays have various choices to do their shopping. Big companies such as eBay and amazon.com have introduced many value added features to help the customers to decide what to shop for. With features such as price comparison, product photos and user reviews, consumers can shop easily without even going to the stores. All they have to do are just browse for the product they want in the website and within a few mouse clicks they are off. Because it is so simple, online shopping attracts many consumers. The question is: why do people still deny shopping online? Well, for most people, privacy and security issues are their concerns.

In the United States, according to a survey, more than half of the adult population uses the Internet, and from that number, about half have shopped online. Studies also showed that privacy and security issues are vital for Internet users to shop online. Most of them regard their personal information as their main concern.

While most consumers trust big and well-established online merchants such as CD Universe and Columbia House, these big companies still receive frequent security threats. Experts also discover that security measures taken by online retailers are insufficient. From this, we can see online shopping is not totally safe.

However, customer rights and security aspects are not just the responsibility of online merchants. To uphold them, the consumers themselves need to act. As the prominent method of payment is credit card, consumers should be more aware in handling it.
They should never disclose their credit information via e-mail. Some of the credit card issuers also have some sorts of protection that consumers should apply for. Apart from that, consumers should limit themselves from releasing unnecessary personal information such as age and income to protect their privacy. Also, consumers should always be aware of the security technology used by merchant sites. Lastly, if there are still dissatisfactions, consumers could always report them to consumer-related agencies.

By common sense, anyone who tends to shop online will think twice before they buy anything. People are always conscious about their privacy and security. However, this is not the case in the real world. Even though online merchants have tried their best to improve the security, threats and attacks still prevail. For this reason, consumers should act fast to protect their privacy when shopping online.

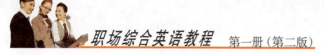

Taking all these contents as a whole, I would say that in any situation, people can still shop online safely if only they understand the reality and take some precautions.

New Words

（标★为A级词汇，标☆为超纲词汇）

★merchant	/ˈmɜːtʃənt/	n.	商人，店主
nowadays	/ˈnaʊədeɪz/	adv.	现今，当今
various	/ˈveərɪəs/	adj.	各种各样的，许多的
comparison	/kəmˈpærɪsən/	n.	比较
browse	/braʊz/	v.	浏览
★website	/ˈwebsaɪt/	n.	网站
click	/klɪk/	n.	（鼠标）点击
deny	/dɪˈnaɪ/	v.	拒绝
concern	/kənˈsɜːn/	n.	顾虑
survey	/ˈsɜːveɪ/	n.	调查
vital	/ˈvaɪtəl/	adj.	至关重要的
☆well-established	/ˈwelɪˈstæblɪʃt/	adj.	信誉卓著的
☆frequent	/ˈfriːkwənt/	adj.	频繁的
retailer	/ˈriːteɪlə/	n.	零售商，零售店
☆insufficient	/ˌɪnsəˈfɪʃnt/	adj.	不足的
aspect	/ˈæspekt/	n.	方面，形势
☆responsibility	/rɪˌspɒnsəˈbɪlɪti/	n.	责任
uphold	/ʌpˈhəʊld/	v.	支持
☆prominent	/ˈprɒmɪnənt/	adj.	重要的
payment	/ˈpeɪmənt/	n.	付款，支付
★credit	/ˈkredɪt/	n.	信用
aware	/əˈweə/	adj.	意识到的
handle	/ˈhændl/	v.	处理；管理；应付
★disclose	/dɪsˈkləʊz/	v.	公开，揭露
★via	/ˈvaɪə/	prep.	经由
issuer	/ˈɪsjuːə/	n.	发行人
☆protection	/prəˈtekʃn/	n.	防护
release	/rɪˈliːs/	v.	公布
income	/ˈɪnkəm/	n.	收入
☆dissatisfaction	/dɪsˌsætɪsˈfækʃn/	n.	不满
★agency	/ˈeɪdʒənsi/	n.	机构
conscious	/ˈkɒnʃəs/	adj.	注意的，关注的
★threat	/θret/	n.	威胁

Unit 4　Online Shopping

★ prevail	/prɪˈveɪl/	v.	（情形、态度、风俗）盛行, 普遍
situation	/ˌsɪtʃuˈeɪʃn/	n.	情况, 局面
★ reality	/rɪˈælɪti/	n.	现实
★ precaution	/prɪˈkɔːʃn/	n.	预防措施

Phrases and Expressions

apply for	申请
apart from	除此之外
as a whole	总体上；作为一个整体来看
if only	只要

Proper Names

eBay	易趣网
amazon.com	亚马逊网
CD Universe	光盘宇宙（光盘销售网站）
Columbia House	哥伦比亚之屋（光盘销售网站）

Exercises

I. Reading Comprehension

Directions: Answer the questions or complete the statements by choosing A, B, C, or D according to the text.

1. According to this passage, there are _____.
   A. more and more online merchants
   B. more and more dangers online
   C. about half American adults shopping online
   D. more requirements customers should know when shopping online

2. People like shopping online because _____.
   A. they are unaware of the dangers existing in online shopping
   B. they don't think it is unsafe to shop online
   C. it is very convenient and takes little time to shop online
   D. there are quality products to buy online

75

3. Why do many people deny shopping online?

   A. Because they like the atmosphere in shops.

   B. Because they are concerned about their privacy and security.

   C. Because there are not enough products to browse.

   D. Because they don't believe online merchants.

4. Online shopping is not totally safe because _____.

   A. online retailers are dishonest

   B. security threats exist everywhere

   C. consumers don't believe online merchants

   D. the security measures are not really available

5. In order to enjoy shopping online we should _____.

   A. never release our credit information, age, or income, and always be aware of the security technologies offered by merchants sites

   B. send as little personal information as possible via email

   C. try not to use credit cards but pay in cash

   D. inform consumer-related agencies about the products we buy online

II. Identifying Pictures

Directions: Match the items shown below with proper English expressions. You can consult your partner or your dictionary, if you have difficulty in understanding any of the English expressions.

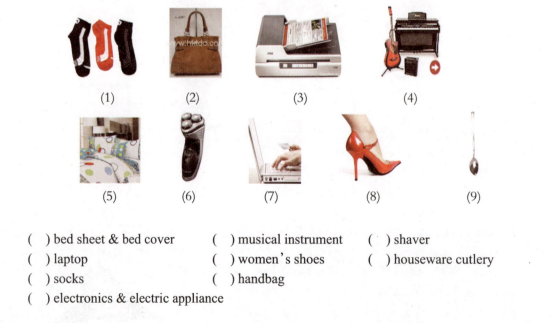

(1)   (2)   (3)   (4)

(5)   (6)   (7)   (8)   (9)

( ) bed sheet & bed cover   ( ) musical instrument   ( ) shaver
( ) laptop   ( ) women's shoes   ( ) houseware cutlery
( ) socks   ( ) handbag
( ) electronics & electric appliance

III. Blank filling

Directions: Use the following words or expressions in the box to translate parts of the following sentences.

try one's best to	tend to	apply for	apart from
regard... as...	even though	precaution	as a whole
if only		handle	

1. Other studies suggest that people who pay with credit cards spend more and _____ _____ （往往忘记他们花了多少钱）.
2. _____（我们采取了所有措施）to minimize the dangers of our trip.
3. He'll never make a good teacher, as he _____（不知道怎样管理小孩）.
4. If _____（整个发达国家遭受经济衰退）, their purchase power will surely decline next year.
5. Some machines are called robots _____（尽管它们不能移动）.
6. If you give me an opportunity, _____（我会尽力把工作做好）in the shortest time!
7. _____（要是当初有人告诉我们）, we could have warned you.
8. What clothes to wear and which friends to hang out with should _____ （被看作个人选择）.
9. She belonged to a generation where princesses didn't have to do anything _____ _____（除了看起来有魅力）.
10. Have you decided _____（你准备申请哪所大学）?

IV. True or false

Directions: Tell whether the following statements are true or false. Write "T" if the statement is true and "F" if it is false.

_____ 1. It is easy and appealing to do shopping online.
_____ 2. Consumers tend to have more confidence in big and well-established online companies.
_____ 3. Big and well-established online companies receive more frequent security threats.
_____ 4. Customers should also be responsible for their rights and security online.
_____ 5. In the real world, customers are not conscious enough about their privacy and security when shopping online.

Text B

Before Reading:

1. What makes online shopping so fashionable throughout the world? Will you buy things online? Why?
2. Do you have the idea to run an online store? If you have such a store, what name will you give it? And what products will you sell? How will you make your online business a success?

Some Benefits of Online Shopping

Internet has revolutionized the way we do our shopping. Because of the numerous advantages and benefits of shopping online, more and more people these days prefer online shopping over conventional shopping. There are many reasons why I think buying on the Internet is the best choice too.

What are the reasons why online shopping is so fashionable? Given below are some reasons for buying online.

1) **Convenience:** The convenience of this method of shopping is what I like best about it. Where else can you do shopping even wearing your night suit? You do not have to wait in a line or wait till the shop assistant is ready to help you with your purchases. You can do your shopping in minutes. Online shops give us the opportunity to shop 24 hours a day and 7 days a week.

2) **Better Prices:** Another thing which fascinates me is the cheap deals and better prices I get from online stores because products come to you directly from the manufacturer or seller without middlemen involved.

3) **Variety:** The choices you can get for products are amazing. One can get several brands and products from different sellers at one place. When you shop online, you can shop from retailers in other parts of the country or even the world without being limited by geographic area. These stores offer a far greater selection of colors and sizes than you will find locally.

4) **Sending Gifts:** Online shopping makes sending gifts to relatives and friends easy, no matter where they stay. Now there is no need of making an excuse for not sending a gift on occasions like birthday, wedding anniversary, marriage, or Valentine's Day.

5) **Fewer Expenses:** Many times when we do conventional shopping we tend to spend more than the required shopping expenses on things like eating out, or traveling.

6) **Comparison of Prices:** Online shops make comparison and research of products and prices possible. Online stores also give you the ability to share information and reviews with other shoppers who have firsthand experience with a product or retailer.

7) **Crowds:** Usually people would like to avoid the crowds when they go shopping. Especially during festivals the crowds can really give a headache. Crowds force us to do a hurried shopping most of the time. Crowds also create a problem when it comes to finding a parking place nearby.

8) **Compulsive Shopping:** Many times when we go out on shopping we end up buying things which we do not require because of the shop keepers' outstanding selling skills.

So, what do you think? Have I not given enough reasons on why online shopping is the best?

Unit 4　Online Shopping

New Words

（标★为A级词汇，标☆为超纲词汇）

☆revolutionize	/ˌrevəˈluːʃənaɪz/	v.	使发生巨大变革
★numerous	/ˈnjuːmərəs/	adj.	数不清的
advantage	/ədˈvɑːntɪdʒ/	n.	优势
☆conventional	/kənˈvenʃənl/	adj.	传统的
fashionable	/ˈfæʃnəbl/	adj.	流行的
suit	/sjuːt/	n.	（从事特定活动时穿的）成套服装
★assistant	/əˈsɪstənt/	n.	店员
purchase	/ˈpɜːtʃəs/	n.	买到的东西
opportunity	/ˌɒpəˈtjuːnɪtɪ/	n.	机会
deal	/diːl/	n.	交易
☆manufacturer	/ˌmænjuˈfæktʃərə/	n.	制造商
middlemen	/ˈmɪdlmæn/	n.	中间商，经销商
involve	/ɪnˈvɒlv/	v.	涉及，包含
☆geographic	/ˌdʒiːəˈɡræfɪk/	adj.	地理的
★selection	/sɪˈlekʃn/	n.	选择
locally	/ˈləʊkəlɪ/	adv.	在本地
gift	/ɡɪft/	n.	礼物
relative	/ˈrelətɪv/	n.	亲属
★occasion	/əˈkeɪʒn/	n.	场合
★anniversary	/ˌænɪˈvɜːsərɪ/	n.	周年纪念日
marriage	/ˈmærɪdʒ/	n.	结婚
expense	/ɪksˈpens/	n.	费用
require	/rɪˈkwaɪə/	v.	需要
research	/rɪˈsɜːtʃ/	n.	调查
firsthand	/ˈfɜːstˈhænd/	adj.	亲身的
avoid	/əˈvɔɪd/	v.	避开
especially	/ɪˈspeʃəlɪ/	adv.	尤其
★festival	/ˈfestɪvl/	n.	节日
force	/fɔːs/	v.	迫使
nearby	/ˈnɪəbaɪ/	adj.	附近
☆compulsive	/kəmˈpʌlsɪv/	adj.	难以抑制的
outstanding	/ˌaʊtˈstændɪŋ/	adj.	出众的

Phrases and Expressions

no matter where	无论在哪里
when it comes to	当提到……；当涉及……
end up	以……结束

Proper Names

Valentine's Day	情人节

Exercises

I. Summary

Directions: Fill in the blanks with the appropriate words according to your understanding.

Online shopping is now very (1) _____. There are many reasons people like online shopping. Firstly, online shopping is very (2) _____. People can shop at home, without waiting in a (3) _____ till the shopper helps out, and even wear their (4) _____. Secondly, online shopping offers people cheaper deals and better (5) _____ because products are sold without middlemen (6) _____. Thirdly, the products you can buy online are really various. You can get several (7) _____ and products from (8) _____ sellers. You can even shop from (9) _____ living in other countries. Fourthly, online shopping means you will not necessarily spent extra money on things like (10) _____, or traveling. The other reasons include comparison of prices, avoiding crowds, etc.

II. Comprehension Based on the Text

Directions: complete the following two statements based on the text.

1. Online shops not only provide comparison and research of products and prices but also the possibility to _____ with other shoppers.
2. When shopping, we sometimes find ourselves buying things we don't actually need just because of the shop keeper's _____.

Unit 4   Online Shopping

III. Vocabulary & Structures

Directions: Choose the proper words or expressions in the box and fill in the blanks.

fashionable	expense	because of	more and more
end up	no matter	when it comes to	occasion
especially	involve		

1. To his own surprise he _____ designing the whole car and putting it into production.
2. She spends _____ time alone in her room.
3. Call me when you get there, _____ what the time is.
4. The car is quite small, _____ if you have children.
5. We bought her the picture on the _____ of her 70th birthday.
6. She looked very _____ yesterday, didn't she?
7. I am still a failure _____ understanding her moods, her strengths and not-so-strengths.
8. The test will _____ answering questions about a photograph.
9. He always gives his children the best no matter what the _____.
10. _____ his long illness, he cannot work very hard now.

IV. Translation

Directions: Put the following English sentences into Chinese.

1. There are many reasons why I think buying on the Internet is the best choice too.
2. Privacy and security issues are vital for internet users to shop online.
3. Where else can you do shopping even wearing your night suit?
4. One can get several brands and products from different sellers at one place.
5. People can shop online safely if only they take some precautions.

Part III Grammar Review

倒装结构

英语句子的主语和谓语有两种顺序：第一种是"主语+谓语"，为自然语序；第二种是"谓语+主语"，为倒装语序。倒装语序又分为全部倒装和部分倒装两种。整个谓语部分都放在主语之前的称为全部倒装，只把谓语的一部分（主要是助动词、情态动词、系动词be等）放在主语之前，其余部分仍在主语之后的称为部分倒装。

1. 全部倒装

1) 以 here, there, now, then, out, in, up, down 等副词开头的句子，其句子主语是名词，谓语是 come, go, stand, live 等动词，这样的句子要求主语部分和谓语部分全部倒装。如：

Here comes the teacher. 老师来了。

There stand two tall trees in front of the gate. 门前有两棵高大的树。

注意：此处，如果主语是人称代词，主语和谓语的语序不变。如：

Here we are. 我们到了。

Away he went. 他离开了。

2) 将表语或地点状语（多为介词短语）置于句首加以强调时，句子的主语和谓语部分要全部倒装。如：

On top of the hill stands a big pine tree. 山顶上耸立着一棵大松树。

Under the tree were some children. 树下有一些孩子。

2. 部分倒装

1) 当某些具有否定意义的副词或状语放在句首时，句子的谓语部分往往采用部分倒装。常见的具有否定意义的词包括：never, neither, nor, little, few, seldom, hardly, scarcely, rarely, in no way, at no time, in no case, by no means, under no circumstance, not only... but also..., no sooner... than..., hardly... when...等。如：

Little did we know that the area is so poor in natural resources.

我们几乎不知道该地区的自然资源是如此的贫乏。

By no means can we allow this to continue.

我们绝不允许这种情况继续下去。

Not only did he come, but also he brought us a lot of presents.

他不但来了，而且给我们带来了很多礼物。

2) Only引导的状语放在句首时，句子的谓语部分要用部分倒装。如：

Only when you told me did I know her name.

直到你告诉我，我才知道她的名字。

Only then did people realize the importance of environmental protection.

直到那时人们才意识到环境保护的重要性。

3) 在以"也"(so), "也不"neither, nor开头的句子中，谓语部分要用部分倒装。如：

He can speak French. So can I. 他会说法语，我也会。

I don't know where he lives. Neither does she.

我不知道他住在哪儿。她也不知道。

4) 虚拟条件句中如果将if省略，则were, had, should提到句首，形成部分倒装。如：

Were I you, I would meet the challenge. 如果我是你，我会迎接挑战的。

Had you followed my advice, you would have finished it early.

要是你听从我的建议的话，你早就完成了。

• Unit 4 Online Shopping •

Assignment 1

Directions: There are eight incomplete statements here. You are required to complete each statement by choosing the appropriate answer from the four choices marked A, B, C, and D.

1. _____ with whom we are familiar.
   A. Here the clown (小丑) comes
   B. Here comes the clown
   C. The clown comes here
   D. Comes here the clown
2. Not until the gasman tells you it's safe _____ turn on the gas again.
   A. you can
   B. can you
   C. you can't
   D. can't you
3. _____ his talk when someone rose to ask him questions.
   A. He has finished hardly
   B. Hardly did he finished
   C. Hardly had he finished
   D. Hardly finished he
4. _____, we got up very early as usual to deliver the newspapers.
   A. As cold was the weather
   B. Cold as the weather was
   C. Cold as was the weather
   D. As the weather was cold
5. You can never use my computer. At no time _____ that machine.
   A. you should touch
   B. touch should you
   C. should you touch
   D. did you touch
6. David's mother seldom does housework on Sunday. _____.
   A. So does my mother.
   B. Nor does my mother.
   C. My mother isn't, either.
   D. My mother doesn't, too.
7. Not until quite recently _____ what a missile was like.
   A. have I known
   B. I have known
   C. did I know
   D. I knew
8. _____, I would have given you his address.
   A. If you asked me
   B. You had asked me
   C. Should you have asked me
   D. Had you asked me

Assignment 2

Directions: Fill in the blanks with proper words.

1. John can speak a little Japanese, and _____ can I.
2. _____ a wonderful performance was it that all the audience clapped warmly.
3. Scarcely had I left _____ it began to rain.
4. Hardly had they settled themselves in their seats in the theater _____ the curtain went up.
5. _____ he here, we would have no difficulty with it.

Part IV Applied Writing

Application Letter（求职信）

求职信的格式和语言都比较正式,语气谦虚有礼、不卑不亢,对自己的能力应客观叙述,不要夸大其词。求职信的目的首先在于获得面试机会,内容不宜过长,以不超过一页为宜。一般来说,求职信应包含以下内容:

1. 介绍信息来源及所要应聘的职位;
2. 表明自己的求职心愿,写信的原因和目的;
3. 说明自己了解应聘职位的要求并满足招聘条件,简要说明自己的学习和工作经历;
4. 摆出其他优势和特长;
5. 简要列出证明人及其联系方式;
6. 感谢对方审阅自己的个人简历,并提出希望得到面试机会。

Sample 1

April 6th, 2017

Dear Sir/Madam,

　　I would like to be considered for the position of Network Maintenance Engineer, as advertised in the local newspaper this evening. Your advertisement interests me because the position that you described sounds exactly like the kind of job I am seeking.

　　I will graduate from Hefei Vocational College in June this year with a diploma (毕业证) in Computer Science. My major is computer system control. Not only have I passed CET-4, but more importantly I can communicate effectively in English.

　　I would appreciate you taking time to review my enclosed resume and if there is any additional information you require, please contact me at xxxx (phone number or E-mail address). I am looking forward to an opportunity to meet with you for an interview.

Yours faithfully,
Jim Hill

Sample 2

June 12, 2017

Dear Sir,

  Your advertisement for a network program designer in China Daily of June 8 has interested me greatly because your requirements closely match my interest and work experience.

  I believe that my education and work experience will make me a qualified candidate for the position. I have earned computer proficiency, a CET-6 certificate and a law school certificate (self-taught).

  My reason for applying this job is to seek greater opportunity for career advancement in a company with outstanding international reputation like yours.

  Mr. Henry Brown who works in your company knows me well and is willing to be my referrer to provide further information about my qualification and suitability.

  You will find an enclosed resume, the school transcript and two copies of reference in this letter. I would really appreciate an opportunity for an interview at your convenience. Please contact me at xxxx (phone number or E-mail address or any contact information).

Yours sincerely,
Peter Tuck

◆ **求职信常用句型**

In reply to your advertisement in (the newspaper) of September 7 for a clerk, I would like to offer myself for the position.
从9月7日(报上)得知贵公司招聘一位职员,我特就该职提出申请。

I am applying for the post of ... advertised in ...
本人欲申请刊登在……上的……一职

... told me that you have a vacancy for ...
……告诉我贵单位有个职位空缺

I look forward to the opportunity of an interview.
期盼得到面试的机会。

I hope you will give my application a consideration.
望您能仔细考虑我的申请。

I have a fair knowledge of ... and I would like to be considered for the position.
我有……方面的经验,请您考虑我是否有资格胜任此职。

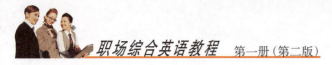

Assignment

Directions: This part is to test your ability to do practical writing. You are required to write an application letter according to the following Chinese instructions.

说 明：

假定你叫刘一鸣，请写封求职信。求职信内容包括：
1. 从2016年12月18日《中国日报》上获悉BAC公司招聘销售部经理职位的信息；
2. 毕业于北京商业技术学院，获得各类证书；曾在DDF公司兼职；
3. 随信附上简历；
4. 希望能获得面试机会。
5. 写信日期：2016年12月20日

Words for reference

《中国日报》	*China Daily*
工商管理	Business Administration
证书	certificate
附上	enclose

Part V Cultural Express

Students Start Online Grocery Store

Belmont（田纳西州贝尔蒙特大学）students Jonathan Murrell and Bruno Silva are delivering groceries to students' dorm rooms through their online care package business that aims to save students time and money.

The friends, both juniors on Belmont's tennis team, joined Murrell's brother James to begin MyDormFood.com last fall. The company delivered some 60 packages in the winter. This fall, MyDormFood.com hopes parents will use its services to send custom-made care packages to their children and students choose the door-step deliveries over off-campus trips and expensive convenience stores.

"One of my friends was getting in the car and eating a PowerBar（一种补充能量的小零食）. She said she paid $3 for it, and I knew it cost half as much at the grocery store. I realized college students were paying super high prices just because of the convenience of having stores on or near campus," said Jonathan. "MyDormFood is identical to grocery store prices. But using us will save time because you don't have to leave your dorm room."

Bruno, James and Jonathan own equal parts of the company, each contributing $2,000 to get their business rolling. Belmont's Center for Entrepreneurship awarded Bruno and Jonathan with the 2011 Outstanding Student Entrepreneur of the Year Award and $5,000.

They do their business at Murrell family's home where basement walls are stocked with all kinds of snack foods, beverages, medicines, personal hygiene products and other dorm essentials from retail warehouse clubs. Customers can go online and select individual products to create their boxes to be delivered to residence halls nationwide.

A lot of businesses begin in a bedroom or the basement of a home. It is really hard to get money in the beginning. This summer, they have used online advertisements and direct mailing to parents as well as on-campus representatives to appeal to students. They are recruiting students at other universities across the country to give them a presence （进驻）at schools outside of Tennessee. The campus representatives hand out promotional flyers and receive a commission（佣金）based on the usage of their discount codes. MyDormFood.com already has connections at other universities and colleges in Tennessee.

"It is difficult to do much marketing on campus," Jonathan said. "But sending packages to the mail room, anyone can send mail. We are just saving parents and students' time and money."

He has taken a leave from Belmont tennis to oversee MyDormFood.com's website, customer service and products. Bruno, a junior studying international business and finance, handles the company's accounting and inventory. James graduated from Lipscomb in May with a degree in marketing.

拓展词汇

购物网站

eBay (www.ebay.com) 易趣；
amazon (www. Amazon.com) 亚马逊；
taobao (www.taobao.com) 淘宝；
dangdang (www.dangdang.com) 当当；
joyo (www.joyo.com) 卓越；
jingdong shopping mall (www.360buy.com) 京东商城

网购常用

e-commerce 电子商务；online shopping 网购；login 登录；logout 退出；bricks and mortar retailer, physical retail store 实体店铺；virtual store 虚拟店铺；shopper 买家；vendor 卖家；shipping charge 运费；item 宝贝；manager 掌柜；customer service 客服

我是卖家

fixed price 一口价；cash on delivery 货到付款；returns 退货；dispatch 发货；packing 包装；out of stock 无现货；in stock 有现货；free shipping, free delivery 包邮；authentic 正品；ten times' pay if found fault 假一赔十；7 days money back or item exchange 七天退换；100% positive feedback 100% 好评

我是买家

bid 出价；watch list 收藏夹；cart 购物车；buyer pays return shipping 买家支付退回邮费；verify the goods 确认收货；give an evaluation rate 信用评价

● Unit 4　Online Shopping ●

网购服务

pay by e-bank 网上银行付款；auction 拍卖；instant kill 秒杀；member activities 会员活动；flash sale 限时抢购；return and exchange policy 退换货政策；buyer 买手；purchasing agent 代购

网购风险

identity theft 身份盗用（指窃取他人个人信息以使用其银行账户等）

89

Unit 5

Advertisements

Learning Objectives

You are able to:

☞ Appreciate advertising slogans

☞ Create an advertisement

☞ Talk about TV commercials

☞ Comment on the advantage and disadvantage of advertising

☞ Listen for key words and useful expressions

☞ Learn to use subjunctive-mood correctly

☞ Write an e-mail

You are suggested to:

☞ Be familiar with some famous advertising slogans

☞ Get to know some renowned brands

• Unit 5　Advertisements •

Part I　Listening and Speaking

Warm-up

Task 1

Directions: Do you know what brands these pictures are advertising? You are allowed to consult the Internet or your partner if you have any difficulties in identifying the brand names.

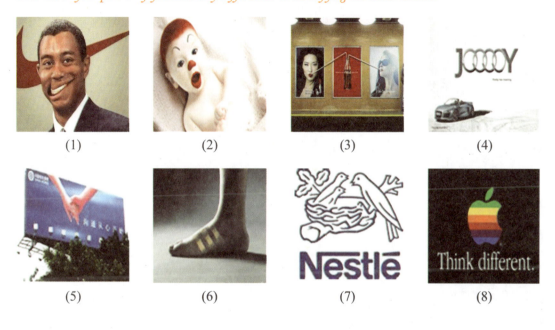

(1)　　　　(2)　　　　(3)　　　　(4)

(5)　　　　(6)　　　　(7)　　　　(8)

Nike	Audi	Coca–Cola	MacDonald's
Adidas	China Mobile	Apple	Nescafé

Task 2

Directions: Have you ever heard the following slogans? Work with your partner and match the slogan with the corresponding products.

百事可乐 ☆　　　　★ Good to the last drop.
诺基亚 ☆　　　　　★ We lead. Others copy.
理光复印机 ☆　　　★ Ask for more.
索尼影碟机 ☆　　　★ Start ahead.
飘柔 ☆　　　　　　★ Connecting people.
麦斯威尔咖啡 ☆　　★ Let's make things better.
飞利浦 ☆　　　　　★ The new digital era.
高露洁牙膏 ☆　　　★ Focus on life.
奥林巴斯 ☆　　　　★ Good teeth, good health.

Oral Practice

Task 1

Directions: Read and practise the following dialogue with your partner, then mark the following statements with "T" or "F" according to what you have read.

Peter: Look, "Make yourself heard!" The Ericsson's TV commercial is so cool.
Jane: I think the Nokia's commercial is just as fascinating: "Connecting People."
Peter: I'm afraid consumers will have to pay for the advertising.
Jane: I hear that the advertisements create a favorable image of a product, and that leads to consumer brand loyalty.
Peter: Could you explain "consumer brand loyalty"?
Jane: I mean consumers identify with the product and keep buying it. Sometimes they're even willing to pay more.
Peter: It is contradictory that increased sales lead to a lower production cost per unit, but more advertising results in greater costs for consumers. The winner is always the company.
Jane: I agree.

• Unit 5   Advertisements •

_____ 1. Jane and Peter are talking about advertisements which they have seen on the street.
_____ 2. Peter thinks that advertising will raise the price of products.
_____ 3. Jane thinks that advertising can help manufacturers increase the sales of their products.

Task 2

Directions: Use the information given below to create a role-play.

Divide the whole class into four groups. Ask each group to choose an item that is for sale at the department store, such as a TV set, computer, cell phone, cosmetics, toys, clothing and etc., and then prepare a TV commercial of that item for the class presentation.

Listening Practice

Task 1

Directions: Now you will hear five short conversations. They will be read only once. After each conversation, there is a question. Listen carefully and choose the best answer from the four choices.

1. ☐ It's not as good as what the ad. says.
   ☐ He doesn't believe it's good for everyone.
   ☐ It's better than what the ad. says.
   ☐ It's good to believe ads.
2. ☐ Husband and wife.   ☐ Teacher and students.
   ☐ Interviewer and interviewee.   ☐ Boss and employee.
3. ☐ It's necessary.   ☐ It's cheap.   ☐ It's widespread.   ☐ It's quick.
4. ☐ He spends too much money on ads.
   ☐ He likes watching ads.
   ☐ He often watches TV programs.
   ☐ He only watches ads on TV.
5. ☐ She went to it on the way to the hospital.
   ☐ She bought something there for her uncle.
   ☐ She missed it.
   ☐ She is not interested in it.

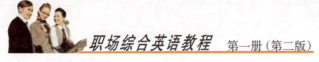

Task 2

Directions: Now you will hear a long conversation. It will be read twice. Then you are required to answer the following questions by making correct choices.

1. What does the man want to do?
   □ Turn off the TV.   □ Switch to another channel.
2. What does the woman praise?
   □ The L'Oreal commercial.   □ The Adidas TV ads.
3. What is the man's attitude to commercials?
   □ He doesn't trust it.   □ He trusts it very much.

Task 3

Directions: Now you will hear a short passage. It will be read three times. Then you are required to put in the missing information.

One day just before closing time, John rushed into a TV store to buy _____ with the money he had saved for three months. The friendly shop assistant was waiting for the day's _____ customer to reach his sales target for his bonus, so he warmly greeted John and showed him the _____ on display. He asked John to see how sharp and colorful the image on the screen was. At that moment, a new commercial _____ the screen, introducing a popular brand of _____ as well as some beautiful pictures it had taken. The camera and the pictures attracted John. He suddenly changed his mind and told the shop assistant: "Thank you for the TV commercial. Now I have to _____ the camera store to get that camera."

New Words and Expressions

commercial	/kəˈmɜːʃl/	n.	（电视、广播中的）商业广告
fascinating	/ˈfæsɪneɪtɪŋ/	adj.	迷人的，有极大吸引力的
consumer	/kənˈsjuːmə/	n.	消费者，用户
favorable	/ˈfeɪvərəbl/	adj.	称赞的，赞同的；有利的
image	/ˈɪmɪdʒ/	n.	印象，形象，影像，图像，肖像
brand	/brænd/	n.	商标，品牌
loyalty	/ˈlɔɪəlti/	n.	忠诚，忠心
identify	/aɪˈdentɪfaɪ/	v.	认出，鉴定；认同
contradictory	/ˌkɒntrəˈdɪktəri/	adj.	相矛盾的
channel	/ˈtʃænl/	n.	频道
advertiser	/ˈædvəˌtaɪzə/	n.	广告商，广告客户
bonus	/ˈbəʊnəs/	n.	奖金，红利
popular	/ˈpɒpjələ/	adj.	流行的，广受欢迎的
attract	/əˈtrækt/	v.	吸引，引起……的注意
on display			展出，展示，陈列

• Unit 5　Advertisements •

Part II　Reading

Text A

Before Reading:

1. In our modern life, advertisements are everywhere. When you watch TV programs, there are advertisements. When you go shopping, there are advertisements. When you surf the Internet, advertisements are ready to pop out here or there. Even when you travel in a remote rural area, advertisements are on the walls of buildings or on the mountainside welcoming you.

   Are you familiar with the following advertisements? What are they about?

(1)　　　　(2)　　　　(3)　　　　(4)

(5)　　　　(6)　　　　(7)　　　　(8)

2. Read the following statements and mark your choices.
   - ☐ Like watching advertisements　　☐ Like the music used in advertisements
   - ☐ Buy the products advertised　　☐ Admire the models in advertisements
   - ☐ Pay no attention to advertisements　☐ Don't believe in ads

The Most Effective Advertising of All

　　Word of mouth advertising is more **effective** than any other form of advertising. People believe what their friends and neighbors say about your company, and they remember it for a longer time. Your company generates word of mouth advertising, whether you know it or not. People are talking about you.

95

The basis of all positive word of mouth advertising is providing superior products and services. This is, in fact, the basis for success with all of your marketing and advertising activities. Happy customers will notice and read your ads. Your advertisements act as positive reminder of your great products and services.

But no company is perfect. It is a fact that very few people will complain — to you. They simply share their experience and their opinion with their friends and family. If they are really unhappy, they will tell everyone they know.

I know a young woman who was not happy with her automobile, and she could not get satisfaction from the dealership. So she printed a large sign on the back of the car that read "I hate my (car name)".

It is hard to imagine a more effective way to ruin a car's reputation. Other drivers beeped and waved. Everyday, every mile, every minute, irreparable damage was done to the car company's reputation. A mad consumer is really a very bad enemy to have.

Yet, if you had a customer with a problem, you would probably act to resolve it, and satisfy the customer. And that would be the best thing to do, because customers who have problems that are satisfactorily resolved are far more likely to be loyal, and to say good things about your company. So getting your customers to complain is a big part of replacing negative word of mouth advertising with positive word of mouth advertising.

Make it as easy as possible for your customers to complain. Instruct your salespeople to ask about problems. Make feedback and comment forms easily available, or include them in billings or at the cash register. Give feedback forms at the table, or after the service has been completed. You need to know how you are doing, and what the complaints or problems are. Think of complaints as opportunities to improve your products and services.

Complaints are a great way to learn about what your customers are thinking and feeling. Complaints will give you new ideas, improve your customer service, and make you a stronger company.

A broken promise is a hard thing to fix. The best strategy is to encourage your people not to over-promise. And if you must break a promise, inform the client as fast as possible. Customers really are very forgiving. They will say nice things about you just because you were polite enough to call them and apologize.

And best of all, fixing problems will lead to loyal customers that spread positive word of mouth advertising for you.

Unit 5 Advertisements

New Words

(标★为A级词汇,标☆为超纲词汇)

effective	/ɪˈfektɪv/	adj.	有效的,起作用的
basis	/ˈbeɪsɪs/	n.	基础;原因;要素
★superior	/sjuˈpɪərɪə/	adj.	(级别、地位)较高的
reminder	/rɪˈmaɪndə/	n.	提示信
★automobile	/ˈɔːtəməbiːl/	n.	汽车
☆dealership	/ˈdiːləʃɪp/	n.	代理权,经销权;代理商
ruin	/ˈruːɪn/	v.	破坏,毁灭
★reputation	/ˌrepjuˈteɪʃn/	n.	信誉;名气,名声
beep	/biːp/	v.	朝某人按车喇叭,嘟嘟响
☆irreparable	/ɪˈrepərəbl/	adj.	不能修复的,不可弥补的
resolve	/rɪˈzɒlv/	v.	决定,解决
replace	/rɪˈpleɪs/	v.	替换,代替
negative	/ˈnegətɪv/	adj.	消极的,否认的
positive	/ˈpɒzətɪv/	adj.	积极的;自信的;建设性的
instruct	/ɪnˈstrʌkt/	v.	教,指导
salespeople	/ˈseɪlzpiːpl/	n.	销售人员
feedback	/ˈfiːdbæk/	n.	反馈
comment	/ˈkɒment/	n.	评论
billing	/ˈbɪlɪŋ/	n.	账单
complete	/kəmˈpliːt/	v.	完成
★complaint	/kəmˈpleɪnt/	n.	抱怨
★strategy	/ˈstrætədʒɪ/	n.	策略,战略
encourage	/ɪnˈkʌrɪdʒ/	v.	鼓励
over-promise	/ˌəʊvəˈprɒmɪs/	v.	过分承诺
★client	/ˈklaɪənt/	n.	顾客;当事人
apologize	/əˈpɒlədʒaɪz/	v.	道歉
spread	/spred/	v.	(使)传播;(使)散布

Phrases and Expressions

act as	充当;扮演
cash register	收银机,现金出纳机

Exercises

I. Reading Comprehension

Directions: Answer the questions or complete the statements by choosing A, B, C, or D according to the text.

1. According to this text the most effective advertising is _____.

    A. the advertisement on television

    B. word of mouth advertising

    C. a large sign on the back of a young woman's car

    D. a bill board (广告牌) put up beside the street

2. Word of mouth advertising _____.

    A. has no effect on the sale of a company's products

    B. affects a company's production

    C. helps a company to provide better products

    D. can be positive or negative to a company's business

3. What will customers do when they are not satisfied with a product or service?

    A. They will complain to the sales managers of the company.

    B. They usually tell the people they meet.

    C. They will be silent and never buy the company's products again.

    D. They will put a sign on the back of their car.

4. What should a company do to a customer's complaint?

    A. Solve his or her problem satisfactorily.

    B. Give the customer time to complain.

    C. Exchange the item the customer is not satisfied with.

    D. Return money to the customer.

5. What's the best strategy for the salespeople to deal with complaints?

    A. Don't overpromise.

    B. Accept the complaints and improve the products or services.

    C. Give the customer feedback or complaint forms.

    D. View the complaints as the best way to know customers.

• Unit 5   Advertisements •

II. Identifying Pictures

Directions: Match the advertisement picture with the corresponding product or service. Consult your partner or dictionary, if you have difficulty in understanding the English words.

(1)   (2)   (3)   (4)   (5)

(6)   (7)   (8)   (9)   (10)

( )coffee   ( ) car   ( ) shoe   ( ) tourism   ( ) fruit
( ) bar   ( ) health club ( ) lip stick ( ) camera   ( ) sun glasses

III. Blank Filling

Directions: Use the words or expressions in the box to translate parts of the following sentences.

| comment | encourage | act as | opportunity | whether ... or |
| share | effective | apologize | negative | improve |

1. You will have _____（有机会提任何问题）at the end of the lecture.
2. _____（他的生活质量已经有了很大改善）since that operation.
3. Now we know for sure that the global warming _____（会对健康产生不利影响）.
4. We _____（为这么晚才回复道歉）. It is due to the bad internet connection here.
5. They could also _____（充当保安系统）to provide internet connection to other things in the building.
6. He declined to _____（对公司在技术方面的投资发表评论）investment in technology.
7. He doesn't know _____（她是在法国还是）she's gone to China.
8. The drug industry says its _____（产品对儿童安全而有效）.
9. The conference is a good place to _____（互通信息）and exchange ideas.
10. My parents have always _____（在我选择职业时鼓励我）.

IV. True or False

Directions: Decide whether the following statements are true or false. Write "T" if the statement is true and "F" if it is false.

_____ 1. Word of mouth advertising is as effective as any other form of advertising.

_____ 2. Providing superior products and services is the basis for successful marketing.

_____ 3. Customers usually tell their experience and their opinion to their friends and family.

_____ 4. People will say good things about the company when their problems have been satisfactorily resolved.

_____ 5. The best way to improve the negative word of mouth advertising is to complain to customers.

Text B

Before Reading:

1. Do you know how to write an advertisement? Is the headline of an advertisement very important? (useful words: headline, brief, block letter, color, telephone number, benefits of the service, product, quality, highlight, read, attractive, appeal to, customer)
2. Do you know how to make an advertisement more effective? (useful words: headline, poetic, romantic, charming, picture, view, appealing, music, melodious, color, sound, voice, model, pun words)

How to Create an Advertisement

Creating an advertisement for a product or a service seems to be a difficult task for many. They can sit at the desk, paper and pen in front of them, and have not written a word. Here are some simple steps to get you started.

Begin the ad creation by analyzing your product and consumer. Each ad has to be made specifically for those who are interested in buying the product or using the service, namely the "consumer".

Understand WHO will buy or use your product or service. Search for as much information about consumers as possible. If your product is already in the market you can obtain this information by doing consumer surveys, talking to the sales people, or observing consumer behavior at various stores. If the product has not come into the market, use best guess strategy or existing market information. Thus you will be able to learn who your buyer or user is. For example, if you are selling a pencil, your target audience may be kids, students, women, men or teachers. Are they the users, or buyers? In the case of pencils users, users may be students, while the buyers are parents.

Find out WHAT is so unique about your product. Make sure you find only one strong reason, otherwise you will confuse your reader. This is also sometimes referred to as brand positioning. Look for something that current competitors do not offer or do not openly claim to offer.

Highlight the product benefit.
- Make a list of your product benefits and then rank them in the order of importance to your consumer. Concentrate on the top most benefits.
- Is there a potential desire or need that will create a market for your product? Evaluate the need gap that exists for the product or service.
- The product claim you make should be credible and trustworthy — don't make unbelieving claims that your product can not provide.

Decide HOW to effectively convey the product message. Normally the product benefit is highlighted by using attractive headlines and pictures. For the tone and style of the ad you need to keep your consumers in mind. It should get their attention, be easy to understand, informative, correct in tone and manner and above all entertaining. Words such as "Free", "Extra", "Best", "New" or "Now" are the traditional favorites. For an instant response, use action words such as Call Now, Hurry, Rush. That will work well. Don't forget to include all the information that is required but at the same time don't overload. Keep it simple and short.

Think of when will they buy, how will they shop for it. This will help you decide how, when and where to advertise, what media is the best for you; choices may be local newspaper, web, fliers and many others.

New Words

（标★为A级词汇，标☆为超纲词汇）

★analyze	/ˈænəlaɪz/	v.	分析，解释
namely	/ˈneɪmlɪ/	adv.	即，也就是
obtain	/əbˈteɪn/	v.	获得，赢得
★target	/ˈtɑːgɪt/	n.	（服务的）对象；目标
audience	/ˈɔːdɪəns/	n.	观众，拥护者
otherwise	/ˈʌðəwaɪz/	adv.	否则
confuse	/kənˈfjuːz/	v.	使混乱，使困惑
★position	/pəˈzɪʃn/	v.	安置，把……放在适当位置
competitor	/kəmˈpetɪtə/	n.	竞争者，对手
claim	/kleɪm/	v.	声称，断言
★rank	/ræŋk/	v.	排列

concentrate	/ˈkɒnsntreɪt/	v.	专心于,注意
evaluate	/ɪˈvæljʊeɪt/	v.	评价,估价
credible	/ˈkredəbl/	adj.	可信的,可靠的
trustworthy	/ˈtrʌstwɜːði/	adj.	值得信赖的,可靠的
unbelieving	/ˌʌnbɪˈliːvɪŋ/	adj.	怀疑的
★convey	/kənˈveɪ/	v.	传达,传递
normally	/ˈnɔːməlɪ/	adv.	正常地,通常地
headline	/ˈhedlaɪn/	n.	大字标题
☆informative	/ɪnˈfɔːmətɪv/	adj.	提供信息的,增进知识的,有益的
extra	/ˈekstrə/	adj.	额外的,附加的,特大的
instant	/ˈɪnstənt/	adj.	立即的
overload	/ˌəʊvəˈləʊd/	v.	使超载,超过负荷
flier	/ˈflaɪə/	n.	(产品的)宣传单

Phrases and Expressions

search for	寻找;搜索
find out	找出
make sure	确定
concentrate on	集中精力于
above all	尤其,最重要的是
at the same time	同时

Exercises

I. Summary

Directions: Fill in the blanks with the appropriate words according to your understanding.

Creating an advertisement seems to be a (1) _____ task for many. Before you begin creating an advertisement, you'd better analyze your products and (2) _____ . That is to say, try to know who will buy or use your product or (3) _____ . For example, if you are selling a pencil, you should know who will be your (4) _____ audience. In addition, you should also know what is (5) _____ about your product. Look for something that current (6) _____ do not offer. Make a (7) _____ of your product benefits and (8) _____ them according to their importance. And try to effectively (9) _____ the product message. Then, make clear when and how consumers will buy your product. This will help you to decide how, when and (10) _____ advertise, what media is best for you.

II. Comprehension Based on the Text

Directions: Complete the following two statements based on the text.

1. If your product is already in the market you can _____ information about consumers by doing consumer surveys.
2. Don't forget to include all the information that is required but at the same time don't _____.

III. Vocabulary & Structures

Directions: Choose the proper words or expressions in the box to fill in the blanks.

concentrate on	search for	analyze	be interested in
at the same time	make sure	instant	above all
find out	talk to		

1. With search engines, we can very efficiently _____ specific terms and phrases in the text.
2. I was laughing and crying _____, and I told Peter that if he had any more surprises for me, he should tell me now.
3. We should start early if we want to _____ of getting there in time.
4. When reading, try not to _____ details until you have understood the main ideas.
5. I must _____ him about his habit of getting home late.
6. The movie Mr. Cameron directed last year was an _____ success throughout the world.
7. Some of these elephants had died, and Miss Emily Levy wanted to _____ why.
8. If we _____ what the minister said, we'll find there is nothing really new in it.
9. Some people say that they _____ the newly-built apartments.
10. I should like to rent a house—modern, comfortable and _____ in a quiet location.

IV. Translation

Directions: Put the following English sentences into Chinese.

1. Fixing problems will lead to loyal customers that spread really nice word of mouth advertising for you.
2. Search for as much information about consumers as possible.
3. Make sure you find only one strong reason otherwise you will confuse your reader.
4. The basis of all positive word of mouth advertising is providing superior products and services.
5. Normally the product benefit is highlighted by using attractive headlines and pictures.

Part III Grammar Review

虚拟语气

条件句有两类,一类是真实条件句,一类是虚拟条件句。真实条件句表达的是可能发生的事,在这种条件句中,谓语动词使用陈述语气。虚拟条件句表达的是一种与客观现实不相符或根本不可能存在的情况,在这种条件句中,谓语动词使用虚拟语气。

虚拟语气的句子根据不同的时间有三种不同的结构形式:

类别	条件从句(If) 谓语动词的形式	主句 谓语动词的形式
与现在事实相反	过去时(be用were)	would/should/might/could + 动词原形
与过去事实相反	had + 过去分词	would/should/might/could+have 动词过去分词
与将来事实相反的情况	① 过去式(be用were) ② should/were to+动词原形	would/should/might/could + 动词原形

虚拟语气的用法
① 与现在事实相反的虚拟条件句
If there were anything to tell you, I would tell it to you.
如果有需要告诉你的事,我会告诉你。
If I knew English, I would read the book in the original.
如果我懂英文,我就看这本书的原文了。
If she lived nearer, I should invite her.
如果她住的近些,我就邀请她了。
If he were free, he would help us.
他要是有空的话,他会帮我们。

② 与过去事实相反的虚拟语气
If she had started a little earlier, she might have been in time for the train.
如果她早点出发,她就来得及赶上那趟火车了。
If he had been here, he would have helped you.
如果他来这里的话,他会帮你的。
If you had worked harder at school, you would have got a better job.
要是你那时在学校里多用点功,你早该找个好工作了。
How could I have missed you if you had been waiting at the entrance?
要是你一直在门口等着,我怎么可能会看不见你?

③ 与将来事实相反的虚拟语气

If I should do the experiment, I would do it in some other way.
如果让我做这个实验,我会用别的方法。
If it should rain, the excursion would be put off.
万一下雨,远足就延期。
If he were to come here, he would tell us about it.
如果他要来的话,他会通知我们。

④ 使用混合时间的虚拟语气

如果虚拟条件句涉及的时间与主句表示的时间不一致,谓语动词用什么形式应取决于各自表示的时间。如:

If he had had the operation two years ago, he would be in better health now.
要是他两年前做了手术,现在健康状况会比较好。
(从句的谓语内容与过去事实相反,主句的谓语内容与现在的事实不符。)
If he were free today, we would have sent him to Beijing.
如果他今天有空的话,我们已经派他去北京了。
(从句的谓语内容与现在事实相反,主句的动作与过去的事实不符。)
If we hadn't got everything ready by now, we should be having a terrible time tomorrow.
要是现在还没有准备就绪,明天日子就难过了。
(从句的动作与过去发生的情况相反,主句的动作与将来发生的事实不符。)

⑤ 虚拟语气在某些宾语从句中的用法

在表示建议、命令、请求、要求或愿望等意义的动词后的宾语从句一般使用虚拟语气,其结构是:(should+)原形动词。这类动词包括 advise, ask, command, demand, desire, decide, insist, order, propose, recommend, request, require, suggest 等。如:

The manager of the hotel requests that their guests shouldn't play loud music after 11:00 p.m.
宾馆经理要求客人在晚上11点以后不得高声播放音乐。
The teacher insisted that he (should) learn the vocabulary by heart.
那位老师坚持认为他应该背单词。
They suggested that the shipment be made within ten days.
他们建议十日内装船。
They demanded that the right to vote be given to every adult man.
他们要求给予每个成年人选举权。

⑥ 虚拟语气在某些主语从句中的用法

在形式主语 it 引出的主语从句中,在表示必要、重要或惊奇等内容的形容词之后,句子的谓语动词常使用"(should) + 动词原形"结构。此类形容词主要包括:advisable(可取的,明智的), desirable(合乎需要的), essential(绝对必要的,极其重要的), imperative(必要的,迫切需要的), important(重要的), natural(自然的), strange(奇怪的), vital(极其重要的,致命的)等。如:

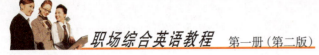

It's important that we (should) learn English well.
学好英语非常重要。

It's quite natural that he should think so.
他那样想很自然。

It's necessary that he be sent there at once.
有必要马上派他去那儿。

It is desired that we get everything ready before Friday.
要求一切在周五前准备好。

Assignment

Directions: There are ten incomplete statements here. You are required to complete each statement by choosing the appropriate answer from the four choices marked A, B, C, and D.

1. Should she come tomorrow, I _____ take her to the museum.
   A. can   B. will   C. would   D. must
2. _____, the police couldn't have had their suspect so quickly.
   A. If the woman didn't record her talk with the attacker
   B. If the woman hasn't recorded her talk with the attacker
   C. Did the woman not record her talk with the attacker
   D. Had the woman not recorded her talk with the attacker
3. _____ more time to think about it.
   A. If only I had   B. Only if I had   C. If I only had   D. Only if had I
4. He demands that we _____ the promise we make.
   A. keeps   B. keep   C. may keep   D. is keeping
5. It was proposed that this matter _____ at the next meeting.
   A. would be considered   B. would have been considered
   C. consider   D. should be considered
6. Those early settlers _____ their first cold winter without the help of their native Indian neighbors.
   A. would not have survived   B. would not survive
   C. could not survive   D. would have survived
7. The committee members suggest that the plan _____ carried out soon.
   A. being   B. been   C. to be   D. be
8. It was essential that all the necessary documents _____ to the dean's office before the end of this semester.
   A. should hand in   B. were handed in
   C. have been handed in   D. be handed in
9. To be frank, I'd rather you _____ in the case.
   A. will be involved   B. not to be involved
   C. not involved   D. were not involved

10. It's already 8:00 p.m. now. Don't you think it's about time _____?
    A. we're going home   B. we go home
    C. we went home   D. we can go home

Part IV Applied Writing

E-mail（电子邮件）

电子邮件,是一种用于社会交往和商务联系的写、送、读全部电子化的信函通讯方式。电子邮件一般由三部分组成:邮件头、正文和签名。

电子邮件的格式和主要内容:

1. 电子邮件必须填写的内容包括:"To"收件人的地址栏,应完整准确地填写;"Subject"主题框的内容应简明的概括邮件的内容,切忌含糊不清。此外,邮件头中常有附件(Attachments),可将要传送的较长的文件,包括文字、照片、图像等,放在电子邮件附件中与邮件同时发出;

2. 电子邮件的正文在结构上与一般信件没有多少区别。正文内容通常较简短,太长的内容可以附件的方式发出。

```
To: _____
Subject: _____


Dear _____,
_____
_____
_____


Best regards,
_____ (signature)
```

Sample 1

To：Zhoutian@sina.com.cn
Subject：China Eastern Flights

Dear Zhou Tian,
Our travel agency here has difficulties in booking domestic flights in China. Could you please arrange for me the following flight on China Eastern Flights, Wednesday, 5th April, Shanghai to Tianjin? I prefer the morning flight. Please confirm with me what flight you have booked, and then I'll finalize my travel details and inform you. Thank you for your help.

Best regards,
Henry

Sample 2

To：Jerry@abc.com
Subject：Studying in U.S.A.

Jerry,
    I hope you did well on your exams last week! I'm very sorry that I didn't answer your e-mail earlier.
    I'm thinking about studying in U.S.A. next year, and I'd like to find out what experiences other people have had. I remember you told me about an e-mail discussion group for students in U.S.A.. Could you tell me how to participate in it?

Thanks!
Li Ming

◆ 电子邮件常用句型

1. I have received your e-mail of Aug.19th. 已收到您8月19日的邮件。

2. I'm glad to have received your e-mail letter. 很高兴收到你的电子邮件。

3. I must apologize for not writing to you for long. 很久没有给你写信,请原谅。

4. I'm very sorry for I didn't answer your message earlier.
   很抱歉没有早点儿回你的信息。

5. I have the pleasure to tell you that... 我很高兴告诉你……

6. Let me know if you'll come as soon as possible! 尽快让我知道你是否能来。

Assignment

Directions: This part is to test your ability to do practical writing. You are required to complete an e-mail according to the following information given in Chinese.

给朋友写一份英文电子邮件,告诉他从开学到现在你对哪一门课程印象最深、最感兴趣,请说出原因。

Part V Cultural Express

Coca-Cola Advertising Stories

Every December I eagerly wait for my first viewing of the Coca-Cola® Christmas advertisement — the one with the Christmas trucks and the jingle that goes, "holidays are coming, holidays are coming ..." You know the one! It isn't Christmas until I've seen that, and I drive my husband crazy asking if it's been on yet. I have to congratulate Coca-Cola on capturing the festive spirit so well, and I look forward to enjoying your advertisement for many years to come.

In the 1950s when I was a little girl there was a calendar that hung behind the meat counter at the grocery store in my neighborhood. It was a Coca-Cola Christmas calendar with Santa holding a long list of good boys and girls. I would stand endlessly searching the list for my name!

In 1976 I lived in South Carolina with my mother who is German and my father who is American. My father was in the U.S. Army, and stationed in Germany, where he met my mother. My mother had applied for her American citizenship twice, but never followed through. In 1975 my mother saw an advertisement for Coca-Cola that stated "Look up America — see what we've got." This ad really touched her heart, and she wrote a letter to the Coca-Cola Company letting them know that, and she went for her third and final time to get her citizenship. Her letter touched the hearts of the people at Coca-Cola and it was used in an advertisement in 1976 in a magazine. The district manager of Coca-Cola and the general manager of the bottling company paid my mother a visit, and gave her an American flag that had flown over the Coca-Cola headquarters in Atlanta, Georgia. I now have the flag and display it proudly, knowing that Coca-Cola had made my mother become the citizen she always wanted to be.

My friends and I were kids and heard that commercial "Coke® Adds Life". We loved the harmony so much that we would all sit out on the porch and sing the song. We would even sing it in the shower because we loved the echo effect that we got in there. We each had our "part" and loved doing it over and over again. That song is what made me realize for the first time that I could sing. It is a great memory to me and I have been a singer ever since then.

My brother and his fiancée are getting married, and I just received their invitation in the mail. My brother and soon-to-be sister-in-law are so into Coke that they decided to incorporate it into their wedding, so the whole wedding is going to be in a Coke theme. They have picked out the song "I'd Like to Teach the World to Sing" because they say that suits them; they are in perfect harmony with each other. Their interest in Coke is what brought them together after all, and they love to just sip on a Coke and enjoy each other's company.

Note:
Coke® Adds Life 可口可乐的广告歌曲
I'd Like To Teach The World To Sing（世界欢乐颂）欧美群星的最新歌曲

Unit 5　Advertisements

拓展词汇

经典英语广告

Just do it. 跟着感觉走。(耐克运动鞋)
Obey your thirst. 服从你的渴望。(雪碧)
Feel the new space. 感受新境界。(三星电子)
Good to the last drop. 滴滴香浓，意犹未尽。(麦氏咖啡)
Started ahead. 成功之路，从头开始。(飘柔洗发水)
Make yourself heard. 理解就是沟通。(爱立信手机)
Intelligence everywhere. 智慧演绎，无处不在。(摩托罗拉手机)
Choice of a new generation. 新一代的选择。(百事可乐)
Where there is a way, there is Toyota. 有路就有丰田车。(丰田汽车)
Let make things better. 让我们做得更好。(菲利浦电器)
Good teeth, good health. 牙齿好，身体就好。(高露洁牙膏)
Can't beat the real thing. 挡不住的诱惑。(可口可乐)
Tide's in, dirt's out. 汰渍到，污垢逃。(汰渍洗衣粉)
Apple thinks different. 苹果电脑，不同凡"想"。(苹果电脑)
Take TOSHIBA, take the world. 拥有东芝，拥有世界。(东芝电子)
No business too small, no problem too big.
没有不做的小生意，没有解决不了的大问题。(IBM公司)
Take time to indulge. 尽情享受吧。(雀巢冰淇淋)
Mosquito bye bye bye. 蚊子杀杀杀。(雷达牌驱蚊剂)
Ideas for life. 为生活着想。(松下电器)

Unit 6

Theme Parks

Learning Objectives

You are able to:

☞ Distinguish theme parks from common parks

☞ Talk about Disneyland

☞ Express your likes and dislikes

☞ Comment on Walt Disney, the man behind Mickey Mouse

☞ Listen for key words and useful expressions

☞ Learn to use passive voice correctly

☞ Write a notice

You are suggested to:

☞ Get to know English expressions of game facilities

☞ Be familiar with some famous organizations in America

• Unit 6　Theme Parks •

Part I　Listening and Speaking

Warm-up

Task 1

Directions: What do you think of theme parks? Try to name the parks in the following pictures. You are allowed to consult the Internet or your partner if you have any difficulties.

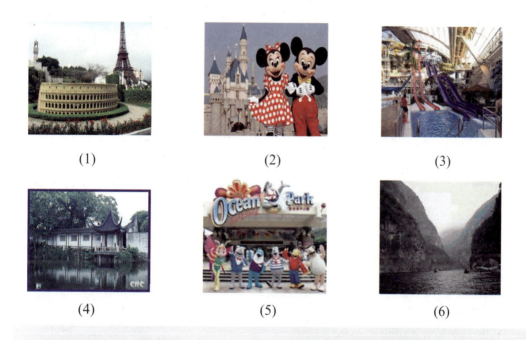

(1)　　　　　　　　(2)　　　　　　　　(3)

(4)　　　　　　　　(5)　　　　　　　　(6)

Hong Kong Ocean Park	A Garden in Suzhou
World Waterpark in Canada	Disneyland
Window of the World in Shenzhen	The Three Gorges of the Yangtze River

Task 2

Directions: The followings are activities we can take in a theme park. Work with your partner and match the Chinese words with corresponding English expressions.

113

海盗船 ☆	★ Bumper car
旋转木马 ☆	★ Roller coaster
摩天轮 ☆	★ Ferris wheel
碰碰车 ☆	★ Pirate ship
云霄飞车 ☆	★ Spook house
鬼屋 ☆	★ Free-fall rides
滑水滑梯 ☆	★ Bungee jumping
卡丁车 ☆	★ Slide
蹦极 ☆	★ Merry-go-round
过山车 ☆	★ Go karts

Oral Practice

Task 1

Directions: Read and practise the following dialogue with your partner, then mark the following statements with "T" or "F" according to what you have read.

Lisa: Have you ever been to Disneyland?

Todd: When I was young, my parents took me to the one in California. But is it Disneyland or Disneyworld, I don't know?

Lisa: The one in Florida is Disneyworld and the one in California is Disneyland, so you must have been to Disneyland.

Todd: That's right. Why do you ask?

Lisa: Well, I've never been to either. So I was thinking of going to Disneyland for my honeymoon.

Todd: When are you getting married?

Lisa: Sometime next month. We haven't set the date yet.

Todd: Congratulations!

Lisa: Thank you. So what do you think?

Todd: Hmm, do you like amusement parks?

Lisa: For the most part, yes. Some of the rides are bit too crazy for me, though.

Todd: If you don't think twice about the rides and go on every ride that you can, you'll have a good time.

Lisa: Even the roller coasters that go through tunnels in the dark?

Todd: Even those. It'll be very exciting, I think. You'll have lots of fun.

Lisa: Thanks for the advice. I'll talk to my fiancé about it tonight.

Todd: I'm sure he'll love the idea. Just throw yourself into it and you'll enjoy it!

• Unit 6　Theme Parks •

_____ 1. Todd went to Disneyworld in California when he was young.
_____ 2. Lisa was thinking of going to Disneyland for her summer vacation.
_____ 3. Todd thinks amusement parks are lots of fun if you could go on every ride that you can.
_____ 4. Lisa will accept Todd's advice to go to an amusement park instead of Disneyland.

Task 2

Directions: Use the information given below to create a role-play.

　　You and your friend are visiting Hong Kong. Now you are discussing where you would like to go tomorrow. Your friend would like to go shopping, but you want to go to the Disneyland. Give reasons for going to Disneyland and persuade your friend to go with you.

Listening Practice

Task 1

Directions: Now you will hear five short conversations. They will be read only once. After each conversation, there is a question. Listen carefully and choose the best answer from the four choices.

1. ☐ She will do her homework.　　☐ She doesn't like Disneyland.
   ☐ She will be with her friends.　　☐ She will see her professor.
2. ☐ Mother and son.　　☐ Father and daughter.
   ☐ Teacher and student.　　☐ Employer and employee.
3. ☐ RMB 600.　　☐ RMB 300.　　☐ RMB 750.　　☐ RMB 450.
4. ☐ On Sunday afternoon.　　☐ On Saturday afternoon.
   ☐ On a weekday.　　☐ On Sunday morning.
5. ☐ He hasn't read about it in the paper.
   ☐ He hasn't watched the news himself.
   ☐ He thinks the news is too good.
   ☐ He heard from the TV news that he shouldn't believe it.

Task 2

Directions: Now you will hear a long conversation. It will be read twice. Then you are required to answer the following questions by making correct choices.

1. What is happening in the dialogue?
   ☐ The speakers are visiting Tokyo.　☐ The speakers are going to Disneyland.
2. What has the man seen before?
   ☐ Hong Kong.　　　　　　　　　☐ Mickey Mouse.

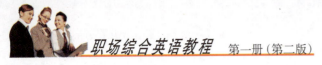

3. What is the man looking forward to the most?
   ☐ Riding the rides.   ☐ Seeing Donald Duck.
4. Where does the dialogue probably take place?
   ☐ In a car.   ☐ In Disneyland.

Task 3

Directions: Now you will hear a short passage. It will be read three times. Then you are required to put in the missing information.

Your first thought of Disneyland might be California, the _____ of the first Disney theme park, opened in _____. And while Disney is largely influenced by the culture of its birthplace, Disney theme parks are spreading around the world.

In 1983 the first _____ Disney theme park opened: Tokyo Disneyland Park in Japan. Tokyo Disneyland Park is now part of the Tokyo Disneyland Resort, and has a _____ Tokyo Disney Sea. Both Tokyo Disneys are _____ by a Japanese corporation, the Oriental Land Company. The Walt Disney Company receives royalties _____ revenues and maintains creative control.

New Words and Expressions

tunnel	/ˈtʌnl/	n.	隧道, 地道
		v.	挖(地道), 开(隧道)
fiancé	/fiˈɒnseɪ/	n.	未婚夫
royalty	/ˈrɔɪəltɪ/	n.	王族(成员) [pl.](著作的)版税
revenue	/ˈrevənjuː/	n.	(大宗的)收入(益); 税收
creative	/kriːˈeɪtɪv/	adj.	创造(性)的, 有创造力的
be influenced by			受……的影响
gonna			<美>将要(=going to)

Part II Reading

Text A

Before Reading:

1. Have you ever been to parks? How do you feel about them? (useful words: beautiful, fresh, interesting, relaxing, refreshing, energetic, happy, joyful, wonderful, trees, lawn, flower, shadow, exciting, dangerous, pavement, etc.)

• Unit 6 Theme Parks •

2. Read the content below and make your choices, and then ask for your partner's choices.
   ☐ prefer water to mountains ☐ prefer mountains to water ☐ like animals
   ☐ like flowers   ☐ like trees and meadow   ☐ like challenging myself

Visiting Theme Parks

One important American contribution to vacation fun is the theme park. Theme parks are a variation on the outdoor entertainment complexes called amusement parks. Like amusement parks, theme parks have games, rides, shows, displays, shops that sell souvenirs, and restaurants and food stands. But theme parks tend to be much larger and more high-tech than the older amusement parks. Furthermore, they are not just outdoor activities in one location, they are developed around a theme or idea, such as American or regional history, marine life, water sports, or African safaris. Many are quite educational as well as entertaining. Theme parks have great appeal to people of all ages and are often a family's primary vacation destination.

Walt Disney, the famous American cartoonist and filmmaker, started it all in 1955 when he opened the first theme park, Disneyland, near Los Angeles, California. Its theme is children's stories, especially those that were made into Disney animated films. Disney's great success inspired the building of parks elsewhere in the U.S. The largest is Walt Disney World, the most popular vacation spot in the world. This complex covers 43 square miles near Orlando, Florida. It includes four major theme parks plus several minor ones. First, there's the Magic Kingdom, which is similar to Disneyland. In addition to the wonderful rides, visitors love its amazing mechanical figures that appear in many exhibits, everything from dancing, singing bears to a life-sized, gesturing, speech-giving Abraham Lincoln. The second park, Epot Center, contains two main sections: Future World highlights technologies of the future; World Showcase features the architecture, food, and entertainment of 11 nations. The third park, Disney-MGM Studios, has Hollywood movie-making as its theme. The newest park—Animal Kingdom—has about 1000 animals, including some rare and endangered ones. The Walt Disney World complex includes four lakes and about 100 restaurants. It's impossible to see and do everything in Walt Disney World, even in several days. A visitor needs two important things—a pair of comfortable shoes and the patience to stand in long lines.

Disney is not the only American company in the theme park business. Six Flags has 14 theme parks and 3 water parks across the U.S. Six Flags Great American has two themes—regions of the U.S. and

117

comic strip characters. Six Flags over Texas focuses on the history of Texas and the U.S. Many theme parks are combinations of amusement parks and zoos. In some, animals roam freely on huge areas of land and tourists drive or ride trains through the territory. Marine animal theme parks have live dolphin shows. Around the country, there are many smaller theme parks built around water activities, where swimmers can cool off on water slides and in wave pools.

New Words

（标★为A级词汇，标☆为超纲词汇）

★contribution	/ˌkɒntrɪˈbjuːʃn/	n.	贡献
☆variation	/ˌveərɪˈeɪʃn/	n.	变化，变动
★complex	/ˈkɒmpleks/	n.	建筑群
★amusement	/əˈmjuːzmənt/	n.	文娱活动
☆souvenir	/ˈsuːvənɪə/	n.	纪念品
high-tech	/ˌhaɪˈtek/	n.	高科技
furthermore	/ˌfɜːðəˈmɔː/	adv.	此外，而且
regional	/ˈriːdʒənl/	adj.	地区的，区域的
☆marine	/məˈriːn/	adj.	海的
☆safari	/səˈfɑːrɪ/	n.	类似游猎的假日旅行
educational	/ˌedʒʊˈkeɪʃənl/	adj.	有教育意义的
appeal	/əˈpiːl/	n.	吸引力；呼吁；恳求
★cartoonist	/kɑːˈtuːnɪst/	n.	漫画家
filmmaker	/ˈfɪlmˌmeɪkə/	n.	电影摄制者
☆animated	/ˈænɪmeɪtɪd/	adj.	活生生的
spot	/spɒt/	n.	地点
★minor	/ˈmaɪnə/	adj.	较小的
★mechanical	/məˈkænɪkl/	adj.	机械的
life-sized	/ˈlaɪfˈsaɪzd/	adj.	（艺术作品）与真人（实物）一样大的
gesture	/ˈdʒestʃə/	v.	做手势
★section	/ˈsekʃn/	n.	部分
☆highlight	/ˈhaɪlaɪt/	v.	强调，突出；把……照亮
architecture	/ˈɑːkɪtektʃə/	n.	建筑风格
rare	/reə/	adj.	罕见的
endangered	/ɪnˈdeɪndʒəd/	adj.	濒临灭绝的
comic	/ˈkɒmɪk/	adj.	喜剧的
combination	/ˌkɒmbɪˈneɪʃn/	n.	联合体
☆roam	/rəʊm/	v.	漫步
★territory	/ˈterɪtərɪ/	n.	领地

Unit 6 Theme Parks

| dolphin | /ˈdɒlfin/ | n. | 海豚 |

Phrases and Expressions

as well as	除……之外(也)
be similar to	与……相似
in addition to	除……之外
focus on	致力于
cool off	变凉；冷却下来

Proper Names

Walt Disney	沃特·迪士尼
Orlando	奥兰多
Disneyland	迪士尼乐园
Walt Disney World	沃尔特·迪士尼世界
Magic Kingdom	梦幻王国
Abraham Lincoln	亚伯拉罕·林肯
Epot Center	未来世界(迪士尼的高科技馆)
Disney-MGM Studios	迪士尼米高梅电影王国
Animal Kingdom	动物王国
World Showcase	世界橱窗
Six Flags	六旗主题公园
Six Flags Great American	美国六旗主题公园
Texas	德克萨斯

Exercises

I. Reading Comprehension

Directions: Answer the questions or complete the statements by choosing A, B, C, or D according to the text.

1. What is the major feature of theme parks?

   A. They provide outdoor activities.

   B. They cover a large area, with high-tech equipments, and have their own themes.

   C. They are designed around a certain historical place and for educational purpose.

   D. They are larger and more attractive than older amusement parks.

2. Where is the first theme park located?

   A. 43 miles near Orlando, Florida.

   B. In Walt Disney World.

   C. Near Los Angeles, California.

   D. Not far from Disneyland.

3. Where can a visitor appreciate amazing mechanical figures when he visits Walt Disney World?

   A. At Animal Kingdom.   B. At World Showcase.

   C. At Magic Kingdom.   D. At Future World.

4. Why does the author say that a visitor to Walt Disney World "needs two important things—a pair of comfortable shoes and the patience to stand in long lines"?

   A. Because it is not allowed to drive in Walt Disney World.

   B. Because you have a long way to walk before you can stand in a line.

   C. Because Walt Disney is very large and too many people like visiting it.

   D. Because uncomfortable shoes will make it hard to stand for a long time in a long line.

5. What does Six Flags have?

   A. Theme parks and water parks.

   B. Amusement parks and history of Texas and the U.S.

   C. Theme parks and zoos.

   D. Amusement parks and water activities.

Unit 6   Theme Parks

II. Identifying Pictures

Directions: Work with your classmates and choose one of the following pictures and describe it.

(1)   (2)   (3)   (4)

(5)   (6)   (7)   (8)

III. Blank Filling

Directions: Use the following words or expressions in the box to translate parts of the following sentences.

be similar to	appeal	focus on	location	endanger
combination	as well as	amazing	territory	destination

1. The president _____ (向公众呼吁) to give blood to the victims of the disaster.
2. _____ (所有相机都对准了) the fashion model as soon as she appeared on the stage.
3. Wolves _____ (有领地) into which other wolves do not usually go.
4. The report found that Australia, New Zealand and America _____ (是年龄较大的旅游者最喜爱的目的地).
5. His teaching style _____ (与其他大多数教师的教学方法相似).
6. Like products and people, _____ (公司的位置和场地) can also be regarded as products.
7. The color purple is a _____ (红色与蓝色的混合体).
8. _____ (除了姓名和地址), the business card should also include the name of your company, your mobilephone number, and your email address.
9. He sang throughout the South, and teenagers went crazy over _____ (他的令人惊奇的声音和吸引人的) performances.
10. That one mistake seriously _____ (危及了公司的未来).

IV. True or False

Directions: Tell whether the following statements are true or false. Write "T" if the statement is true and "F" if it is false.

_____ 1. American contribution to vacation fun is the theme park.

_____ 2. Theme parks are generally larger than the amusement parks.

_____ 3. Walt Disney opened the first theme park, Walt Disney World.

_____ 4. The theme of Disneyland is children's stories, especially those that were made into Disney animated films.

_____ 5. There are many animals, including some rare and endangered ones, living in Magic Kingdom.

Text B

Before Reading:

1. Do you know any famous parks? Use your own words to describe them. (for example: location, view, number of visitors, price)
2. Do you know something about Walt Disney? What made Walt Disney so famous throughout the world?

Walt Disney

Probably no other company has pleased so many children. It is not surprising that it has been called a dream factory. Millions of people have seen Disney films and television programs. They have made friends with all the Disney heroes: Mickey Mouse, Donald Duck, Snow White, Pinocchio, Peter Pan. Millions more have visited the company's major entertainment parks.

Walter Elias Disney was born in Chicago, and in nineteen twenty-three, he decided to make animated movies. In them, drawings are made to move in a lifelike way. We call them cartoons. Disney, the artist, wanted to bring his pictures to life. First he decided he needed a cartoon hero. Because Disney and his partner Ub Iwerks, another young artist, often saw mice running in and out of the old building where they worked, they decided to draw a cartoon mouse. It was not exactly like a real mouse. For one thing, it stood on two legs like a human. It had big eyes and ears. And it wore white gloves on its hands. The artists called him "Mickey". Mickey Mouse appeared in hundreds of cartoons during the years that followed. He became known all over the world. Mickey soon was joined by several other cartoon creatures.

One was the female mouse called "Minnie". Another was the duck named "Donald", with his sailor clothes and funny voice. And there was the dog called Pluto. Many movie experts say Disney's art of animation reached its highest point in nineteen forty with the movie "Pinocchio", which is about a wooden toy that comes to life as a little boy.

In nineteen fifty-five, Walt Disney opened an entertainment park not far from Hollywood, California. He called it "Disneyland". He wanted it to be the happiest place on Earth. Disneyland recreated imaginary places from Disney movies. It also recreated real places—as Disney imagined them. For example, one area looked like a nineteenth century town in the American West. Another looked like the world of the future. Disneyland also had exciting rides. Children could fly on an elephant, or spin in a teacup, or climb a mountain, or float on a jungle river. And—best of all—children got to meet Mickey Mouse himself. Actors dressed as Mickey and all the Disney cartoon creatures walked around the park shaking hands with visitors.

Disneyland was so successful that Disney developed plans for a second entertainment and educational park to be built in Florida. The project, Walt Disney World, opened in Florida in nineteen seventy-one, after Disney's death. The man who started it all, Walt Disney, died in nineteen sixty-six. But the company he began continues to help people escape the problems of life through its movies and entertainment parks.

New Words

（标★为A级词汇，标☆为超纲词汇）

drawing	/ˈdrɔːɪŋ/	n.	绘画
lifelike	/ˈlaɪf ˌlaɪk/	adj.	栩栩如生的
★ cartoon	/kɑːˈtuːn/	n.	漫画
partner	/ˈpɑːtnə/	n.	伙伴
★ glove	/ɡlʌv/	n.	手套
known	/nəʊn/	adj.	已知的
★ creature	/ˈkriːtʃə/	n.	生物
female	/ˈfiːmeɪl/	adj.	女性的；雌的
sailor	/ˈseɪlə/	n.	海员
☆ animation	/ˌænɪˈmeɪʃn/	n.	动画片设计
recreate	/ˌriːkrɪˈeɪt/	v.	重现

☆ imaginary	/ɪˈmædʒɪnərɪ/	adj.	想象中的
spin	/spɪn/	v.	快速旋转
teacup	/ˈtiːkʌp/	n.	茶碗,茶杯
float	/fləʊt/	v.	漂浮
jungle	/ˈdʒʌŋgl/	n.	丛林
escape	/ɪˈskeɪp/	v.	逃脱

Phrases and Expressions

| make friends with | 与……交友 |
| best of all | 最好的是;尤其是 |

Proper Names

Mickey Mouse	米老鼠
Donald Duck	唐老鸭
Snow White	白雪公主
Pinocchio	皮诺曹
Peter Pan	彼得潘
Chicago	芝加哥
Ub Iwerk	布·伊沃克斯
Minnie	米尼
Pluto	普鲁托

Exercises

I. Summary

Directions: Fill in the blanks with the appropriate words according to your understanding.

Disney company has often been called (1) _____. The founder Walter Elias Disney was born in (2) _____. In nineteen twenty-three, he decided to make (3) _____ movies. In these movies, drawings moved in a lifelike way, which we call (4) _____. The first cartoon creature was (5) _____. The following cartoon creatures include the female mouse (6) _____, the duck (7) _____, and the dog Pluto. Later, Walt Disney opened an (8) _____ park. He named this park (9) _____. After Disney's death, a second entertainment park, Walt Disney World, opened in (10) _____ in nineteen seventy-one.

II. Comprehension Based on the Text

Directions: Complete the following two statements based on the text.

1. Because Disney and Ub Iwerks often saw mice running in and out of the old building where they worked, they decided to draw a cartoon mouse. This cartoon mouse is _____.
2. Disneyland was successful. So Disney developed a second entertainment and educational park. It was opened after Disney's death, and its name is _____.

III. Vocabulary & Structures

Directions: Choose the proper words or expressions in the box and fill in the blanks.

best of all	imaginary	funny	exciting	major
decide	make friends with	float	exactly	appear

1. The beaches are beautiful, but, _____, there are few tourists.
2. Over the course of the school year, Anderson became popular and easily _____ other students.
3. He _____ to be your friend but I doubt if he is.
4. The visitors noticed fifty and twenty dollar bills _____ in the water.
5. All the students burst into laughter when Jim walked in wearing his _____ clothes.
6. The doctors held a meeting to _____ whether an operation was necessary.
7. The equator (赤道) is an _____ line around the middle of the earth.
8. Each corner had a guard tower, each of which was _____ ten meters in height.
9. I have been living as an ordinary person. I sometimes dream of an _____ career, like being a spy.
10. Samuel Clemens, who was known as Mark Twain, is a _____ novelist in the history of American literature.

IV. Translation

Directions: Put the following English sentences into Chinese.

1. It is not surprising that it has been called a dream factory.
2. Mickey Mouse appeared in hundreds of cartoons during the years that followed.
3. Theme parks have great appeal to people of all ages and are often a family's primary vocation destination.
4. Disneyland was so successful that Disney developed plans for a second entertainment and educational park to be built.
5. Animals roam freely on huge areas of land and tourists dive or ride trains through the territory.

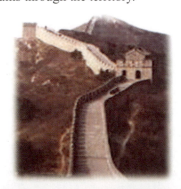

Part III Grammar Review

被动语态

语态有两种：主动语态和被动语态。在句子中使用哪一种语态，取决于句子的主谓语关系。主语所指人或事物如果是谓语所含动作的执行者，即谓语所含动作由主语所指人或事物完成，谓语动词要使用主动语态；反过来，如果主语所指人或事物是谓语所含动作的承受者，即谓语所含动作不是由主语所指人或事物而是由其他人或事物完成，谓语动词应使用被动语态。

被动语态的基本结构是连系动词be+动词的过去分词。连系动词be有多种变化形式，如过去时形式（was和were）和现在完成时形式（has been 和have been）。涉及不同时态时，要用合乎时态要求的变体。

一般现在时被动语态	am, is, are	+	过去分词(-ed形式)
一般过去时被动语态	was, were		
一般将来时被动语态	will be, is going to be		
现在进行时被动语态	am/is/are + being		
过去进行时被动语态	was/were + being		
现在完成时被动语态	have/has + been		
过去完成时被动语态	had been		
现在将来完成时被动语态	will have been		
过去将来完成时被动语态	would have been		
含情态动词的被动语态	can/may/must + be		

1) 一般现在时的被动语态（is / am / are+过去分词）

   Our room is cleaned everyday. 我的房间每天打扫。

   Knives are used for cutting things. 刀子用来切割东西。

2) 一般过去时的被动语态（was / were+过去分词）

   A water power station was built in the area several yeas ago.

   几年前这儿建了一座水电站。

   This picture was taken by a young reporter in Beijing last month.

   这张照片是北京的一位年轻记者上个月拍摄的。

3) 现在完成时的被动语态（has / have+been+过去分词）

   This book has been translated into many languages.

   这本书已被翻译成多种语言。

Many man-made satellites have been sent up into space by many countries.
现在许多国家都能把人造卫星发射到太空。

4) 一般将来时的被动语态（will/shall+be+过去分词）

The goods that you ordered ten days ago will be delivered to you tomorrow.
你十天前的订货明天发送。

It is announced that the lunch time will be shortened from one hour to 45 minutes.
通知说午餐时间要从一个小时减少为45分钟。

5) 过去将来时的被动语态（would/should+be+过去分词）

The work would be finished soon. 这份工作应该不久就可以完成。

They were told that the result would be announced the next week.
他们被告知，结果将在下一周宣布。

6) 现在进行时的被动语态（am／is／are+being+过去分词）

My bike is being repaired now. 我的自行车这会正在修。

The trees are being planted over there. 那边正在植树。

7) 含有情态动词的被动语态（情态动词+be+过去分词）

The door may be locked inside. 这门或许从里面反锁了。

This point should not be neglected. 这一点不可忽视。

Assignment

Directions: There are ten incomplete statements here. You are required to complete each statement by choosing the appropriate answer from the four choices marked A, B, C and D.

1. She was told the examination _____ on Friday.
   A. has been given　　　　　　B. would be given
   C. to be given　　　　　　　　D. is being given
2. The meet didn't taste very good. They _____ for too long.
   A. cooked　　　　　　　　　　B. were cooked
   C. had cooked　　　　　　　　D. had been cooked
3. People _____ to talk loudly in the library.
   A. are allowed　　　　　　　　B. allowed
   C. are not allowed　　　　　　D. don't allow
4. There are many problems _____ in the wide use of solar energy in industry.
   A. being considered　　　　　　B. to consider
   C. will be considered　　　　　D. to be considered
5. Great as Newton was, many of his ideas _____ today and are being modified by the work of scientists of our time.
   A. are challenging　　　　　　B. have been challenged
   C. will be challenged　　　　　D. to challenge

6. A few classroom buildings _____ next to the Lab Building.
   A. is being built   B. have been built
   C. has built   D. will build
7. This novel _____ into three foreign languages.
   A. will being translated   B. has translated
   C. will be translated   D. being translated
8. The work _____ by the time you get there.
   A. would have done   B. is being done
   C. has been done   D. will have been done
9. Visitors _____ not to touch the windows.
   A. being told   B. were told
   C. would tell   D. had told
10. Time _____.
   A. should not be wasted   B. has not wasted
   C. should be not wasted   D. not being wasted

Part IV Applied Writing

Notice（通知）

通知（或称告示）是向大众告知某一事情的简短文字，通常刊登在报刊上或张贴在公共场所。通知可分为书面通知和口头通知两类，书面通知一般包含标题、日期、通知事项、时间、地点、具体要求及落款等内容。口头通知一般只包含通知事项、时间、地点、具体要求等。

通知的主要内容一般包括：
1. 标题 (Notice) 写于正文上方正中；
2. 日期通常写于正文的右上方，有时写在低于落款的左下角；
3. 正文内容具体明确，语言精练，包括事件、时间、地点、具体要求等；
4. 落款处写出发通知的人或单位名称。

Unit 6　Theme Parks

Sample 1

Notice

Dec. 15, 2016

　　College English Test Band-4 is to be held on Saturday Morning (December 17) from 9:00 to 11:15 in the Teaching Building. All the classrooms in that building are then to be used for the test.

　　Students should prepare your pens, 2B pencils, head-phones. Check your test room number and your CET4 candidate number before you enter your test room. Do be there no later than 8:40.

Dean's office

Sample 2

GOOD NEWS!!!
(Winter Clearance Sales)

　　All the goods on show are sold at 20%—50% discount from March 11 to March 20.

　　Warn you in advance:

　　Please examine and choose the goods carefully before you pay. There will be no replacement or refunding.

　　You are welcome.

P&K Shopping Center

◆ 通知常用句型

All are warmly welcome. 欢迎光临！

The meeting will be put off until next week. 会议将推迟到下周。

Please be there/present on time. 请准时参加。

There will be a meeting in the conference room this afternoon. 定于今天下午在会议室召开会议。

It is expected that / be expected to ... 要求……

... be supposed to... ……必须……

... be requested to... ……请……

We are pleased to inform you that... 我们很高兴地通知你……

... only if weather permits. ……遇雨取消或改期。

Assignment

Directions: This part is to test your ability to do practical writing. You are required to write a notice according to the following instructions given in Chinese.

> 通知
>
> 兹定于2016年12月9日星期五下午5:30在会议室开会，请全体教师准时参加。
>
> 教务处
> 2016年12月6日

Part V　Cultural Express

Indoor Water Parks

Theme parks and water parks used to be different from each other. If you wanted to ride coasters（雪橇）and carousels（旋转木马）, you went to the theme park; if you wanted water slide（水滑梯）fun and relief from the heat, you headed to the water park. The idea of combining the two concepts seemed crazy. But not that crazy. After all, water frolickers（嬉戏者）have been riding coasters at traditional seaside and lakeside amusement parks for years.

It used to be that if people in North America who lived anywhere outside of Florida wanted to ride down a water slide during February, they had to wait until June or book a flight to Florida. That's no longer true. Indoor water parks now offer a low-cost alternative to expensive tropical vacations in the winter. And because they are weatherproof, people can have water park fun any time of the year.

The concept began in 1994 when a hotelier in Wisconsin thought that if he had an outdoor water park attraction in his indoor pool, he might be able to get more business in the early spring and late fall. When crowds of guests showed up — and kept showing up straight through the winter—he knew that he was onto something.

The idea exploded in the Wisconsin Dells（威斯康星峡谷）, expanded into the Midwest, and later spread throughout the US (even to Alaska!) and into Canada.

Today there are dozens of indoor water park hotels. But not all parks are created equal. And the biggest ones aren't necessarily the best. Which ones make the biggest splash?

Located just 90 miles north of Pittsburgh（匹兹堡）, Pennsylvania, the Splash Lagoon resort complex includes Splash Lagoon Indoor Water Park, Laser Tag Arena and Arcade, and several hotel properties connected to the water park. The indoor water park features the latest and greatest rides in the water park industry, set in a South Sea Island atmosphere with palm trees, tropical plants, and flowers.

Imagine 365 days of 84-degree temperatures. Now imagine that same year-round balmy weather! Enter Splash Lagoon, Pennsylvania's only indoor water park—sure to turn even a bad cold day into a warm tropical paradise. There adults can float down a lazy river while the kids twist and turn down numerous slides. Plus, enjoy body coasters, tube coasters, and an 80,000 gallon activity pool. Splash Lagoon is a good-size indoor water park with a great assortment of slides and water attractions. Its colorful tropical theme offers a warm and inviting ambiance. The park's centerpiece is the Tiki Tree House, which includes a huge tipping bucket, a couple of smaller water slides, and a bunch of hoses, sprayers, pumps, and other interactive gizmos（装置）to soak everyone on the play structure. Among Splash Lagoon's unique features, it offers two bowl rides. The Cyclone accommodates one- and two-person tubes, while Hurricane Hole foregoes the tubes and sends riders down a body slide and into its bright orange and yellow bowl. In all, Splash Lagoon Indoor Water Park offers fun for the whole family.

拓展词汇

组织及协会名称

AZA (Association of Zoos and Aquarium) 美国动物园及水族馆协会

IAAPA (International Association of Amusement Parks and Attractions) 国际休闲娱乐与主题公园协会

TEA (Themed Entertainment Association) 美国主题娱乐协会

AALR (American Association for Leisure and Recreation) 美国休闲与游憩协会

APTA (Asia Pacific Tourism Association) 亚太旅游组织

ASTA (American Society of Travel Agent) 美国社会旅行社

ATF (Asia Touring Forum) 亚太旅游论坛

游乐项目

ferries wheel 高空观览车；seesaw 跷跷板；swing 秋千；bumper car 碰碰车；roller-coaster 过山车；merry-go-round 音乐木马；maze 迷宫，迷阵；slide 滑梯；bungee jumping 蹦极跳；strop 滑索；aerate spring 充气弹跳；flying trapeze 空中飞人

游乐设施

merry-go-around type of rides 转马类游艺机
space-gyro type of rides 陀螺类游艺机
fly-tower type of rides 飞行塔类游艺机
wonder wheel type of rides 观览车类游艺机
coaster type of rides 滑行车类游艺机
fairy train type of rides 小火车类游艺机
racing car type of rides 赛车类游艺机
battery car type of rides 电池车类游艺机
sight-seeing vehicle type of amusement devices 观光类游乐设施
shooting gallery type of rides 光电打靶类游艺机
water amusement equipment 水上游乐设施
children recreation castle 儿童娱乐城